The French GCSE Handbook

The complete guide to getting a grade 9

About the author

Lucy Martin was educated in Brussels and the UK and has a First-Class degree in Modern Languages from Wadham College, Oxford. She speaks five languages and teaches to all levels, with a superb track record in top exam results. She is a contributor to BBC Bitesize and has written twelve books of her own for students of French, Spanish and German. She lives in London with her three children.

Third edition

Copyright Lucy Martin 2019

www.lucymartintuition.co.uk

Table of contents

Introduction

In my ten years of tutoring French, I have helped many students get top marks at GCSE, even the ones who came to me a few months beforehand without the slightest clue about any of the grammar basics.

As well as basic grammar revision and sample oral answers, there are also hints and tips for the role play, the reading, writing and listening tasks. The Speaking section, which is also available as a standalone book How to ace your French Oral, contains sample answers on the main topics covered at GCSE, together with English translation and glossary.

It's not cheating! Languages are hard to learn in a classroom, and teachers rarely have enough time to give each student the one-to-one time he or she needs for oral practice. There are plenty of students out there getting help outside school, and this is your chance to be one of them.

The final section of the book contains vocabulary lists set out in topics and including tips on how to remember not just the words themselves but their gender and the prepositions that commonly go with them. Using a mixture of visual clues and imaginary situations I create links that avoid the need for learning by rote.

You may also find it useful to subscribe to my YouTube channel Lucy Martin Tuition where my videos help students understand grammar points and prepare for the speaking and writing exams.

I wish you all success with your language studies and welcome any feedback you may have via my website:

www.lucymartintuition.co.uk

Bonne chance!

PART 1

Grammar

Nouns and Gender

Nouns in French are masculine or feminine.

The indefinite article un, une

The word for "a" or "an" is either **un or une** depending on whether the noun is masculine (un chien – a dog) or feminine (une table – a table). There are a few rules to help you work out the gender of nouns but generally you need to learn each word with its gender.

The definite article le, la, les

The definite article "the" is **le, la or les** but special rules apply to it.

- Use it when we say **the** in English:

  Le for masculine nouns   le chien = the dog
  La for feminine nouns   la maison = the house
  Les for plural nouns   les enfants = the children

- Use it for **generalisations**:

  Dogs are nice   les chiens sont sympas
  Chocolate is delicious   le chocolat est délicieux

- Use it with **school subjects**:

  I am studying history   J'étudie l'histoire

- Use it when talking about **liking, hating, disliking, preferring**

  J'aime **les** chiens   I like dogs
  Je préfère **les** chats   I prefer cats
  J'aime **la** pizza   I like pizza
  J'adore **la** neige   I love snow
  Je déteste **la** viande   I hate meat
  Je n'aime pas **les** documentaires   I don't like documentaries

Adjectives

- **Adjectives go after the noun,** except in a few cases which include: grand, petit, joli, nouveau, vieux, bon, beau, mauvais, gros.

- **They agree** with the noun they are describing. "Il est grand" but "elle est grande" and "elles sont grandes" etc. Adjectives like petit, grand, amusant, bavard, marrant, intelligent take an e for the feminine and an s for plural. Others are more complicated. For a list of adjectives and their feminine forms, look at the vocabulary lists overleaf and in the back of this book.

- **They don't agree after c'est** (it is). After c'est or c'était, the adjective is always masculine.

- **Some don't agree at all!** (see list) usually because they end in an "e" or because the adjective is an abbreviation (sympa), a compound word (casse-pieds).

- Use the **comparative** or **superlative** to improve your mark

plus.............que	more .... than
moins..........que	less .... than
le meilleur collège de Londres	the best school in London
la meilleure ville du monde	the best town in the world

- You can **qualify** your adjective using:

très	very
assez	quite
extrêmement	extremely
parfois	sometimes
toujours	always
un peu	a bit

Common adjectives with their feminine forms

grand(e) / petit(e)	tall / small
gros(se)	fat
bavard(e)	chatty
marrant(e)	funny
intéressant(e)	interesting
embêtant(e)	annoying
joli(e)	pretty
fort(e)	strong
fâché(e)	angry
méchant(e)	naughty
gentil(-le)	kind
ennuyeux/-euse	boring
paresseux/-euse	lazy
sérieux/-euse	serious
heureux/-euse	happy
sportif/-ive	sporty
vieux (vieille)	old
beau (belle)	beautiful
mince	thin
sympa	nice
égoïste	selfish
jeune	young
moche	ugly
agréable	pleasant

"My" and other possessive adjectives

Whereas in English, you say *my* regardless of the noun that follows, in French, the word for *my* varies according to the gender and number of the thing that you own.

mon with masculine nouns   mon chien = my dog
ma with feminine nouns   ma maison = my house
mes with plural nouns   mes parents = my parents

This works with *your* (**ton, ta, tes**) and *his* or *her* (**son, sa, ses**) using the same rule. Remember that there is no separate word for "his" and "her", Both are son/sa/ses, so you will need to determine meaning from the context.

son père   his/her father
sa mère   his/her mother
ses parents   his/her parents
tes amis   your friends
ta sœur   your sister
ton frère   your brother

In the plural forms (our, your and their) there are only two forms

notre père   our father
notre mère   our mother
nos parents   our parents
votre frère   your brother
votre sœur   your sister
vos amis   your friends
leur oncle   their uncle
leur tante   their aunt
leurs grands-parents   their grandparents

If you are using the pronoun *on,* the corresponding possessive adjective is *son / sa / ses*:

Il y a un club où on peut retrouver ses amis.
There is a club where one can meet up with one's friends.

Pronouns

Pronouns stand in the place of nouns. Instead of repeating "my friend Sarah" every time, we use the word "she". When we know what or who we are talking about, we substitute the names of people and objects with words like *he, she, they, it, them, him, her, us, you* etc.

Subject pronouns

Subject pronouns in French are the ones you see in every verb table:

je	I
tu	you (singular)
il	he (or *it*, with masculine nouns)
elle	she (or *it*, with feminine nouns)
on	we / one
nous	we
vous	you (plural)
ils	they (masculine)
elles	they (feminine)

Direct object pronouns

If I say, "I like *it / him*", we need to know how to say *it* or the *him,* which is the object pronoun because it stands in the place of the object of the sentence.

me	me
te	you
le	him (or *it* with masculine nouns)
la	her (or *it* with feminine nouns)
nous	us
vous	you
les	them

Je le vois	I see him / it
Il l'aime	he likes it / him / her
Tu la manges	you eat it (eg. une pomme)
Elle le sait	she knows it
Je les adore	I love them
Il t'aide	he helps you
On le fait	we do it

Indirect object pronouns

Some verbs like donner, dire and demander take an indirect object. Indirect object pronouns are the same as direct object pronouns except *le* and *la* go to **lui** (meaning *to* him or her) and *les* goes to **leur** (meaning *to* them).

Ils lui donnent le livre	They give him/her the book
Elle leur dit bonjour	She says hello to them
Je lui donne le crayon	I give him/her the pencil
Il me demande de partir	He asks me to go

Position of pronouns

The object pronoun goes before the verb, and in the past tense before the auxiliary. In the case of the near future tense, or where a modal verb is being used, the pronoun goes before the infinitive.

Je l'aime	I like it
Il les mange	He eats them
Je vais le faire	I'm going to do it
Il doit le porter	He has to wear it

Agreement of the past participle in the past tense

If the pronoun stands in the place of a plural or feminine noun, the past participle agrees:

Nous les avons mangées	we ate them *(les pommes)*
Il l'a vue	he saw her *(la maison)*
Ils les ont lus	They read them *(les livres)*
Elle les a faits	She has done it *(les devoirs)*
Il t'a vu	He saw you
Nous l'avons bu	We drank it *(le café)*

Verbs

The most important verbs in French: être and avoir

These verbs don't just mean *to be* and *to have*, they are used to form the past tense – or passé composé, so you need to be very familiar with them. To revise them, recite them in a rhythm. Notice how all the *avoir* ones begin with *a* (except *ont*, but the o is almost an a…) and notice how the *sont* and the *ont* rhyme when you recite it. Picture, recite and repeat the two verbs in the order they are below.

être – to be	
Je suis	I am
Tu es	you (singular) are
Il est	he is
Nous sommes	we are
Vous êtes	you (plural) are
Ils sont / elles sont	they are
avoir – to have	
J'ai	I have
Tu as	you (singular) have
Il a	he has
Nous avons	we have
Vous avez	you (plural) have
Ils ont / elles ont	they have

To make them negative, just put **ne……pas** around the verb. But with avoir, if you *don't* have something, use **de** before the noun.

Je ne suis pas sûr	I am not sure
Il n'est pas marrant	He's not funny
Elles ne sont pas là	They aren't there
Tu n'as pas **de** sœur ?	Don't you have a sister?
Elle n'a pas **de** stylo	She doesn't have a pen

Present tense

There are three main types of regular verb in French, ending in –er, -re and –ir. The first half of the first column (er) is **easy** (e / es / e sounds like "easy"). The second column (re) is **so so difficult (s s d)**. The third column (ir) is the LAST so th**is is it**. The second half of each (nous, vous, ils) is **ons ez ent** every time, except for the last column where your batteries are running out, you're slowing down and you're adding sleepy snoring sounds to it **issons issez issent**.

jouer – to play	répondre – to answer	finir – to finish
je joue tu jou**es** il/elle/on joue nous jou**ons** vous jou**ez** ils/elles jou**ent**	je répond**s** tu répond**s** il/elle/on répon**d** nous répond**ons** vous répond**ez** ils/elles répond**ent**	je fin**is** tu fin**is** il/elle/on fin**it** nous fin**issons** vous fin**issez** ils/elles fin**issent**
similar verbs: *écouter – to listen* *habiter – to live* *manger – to eat* *parler – to speak* *aimer – to like* *aider – to help* *chanter – to sing* *dessiner – to draw* *nager – to swim* *danser – to dance* *laver – to wash* *ranger – to tidy* *porter – to wear* *bavarder – to chat* *voyager – to travel*	similar verbs: *vendre – to sell* *descendre – to go down* *entendre – to hear*	similar verbs: *vomir – to be sick* *choisir – to choose*

Irregular verbs in the present tense

There are a lot of irregular verbs in French but here are some of the most useful ones. Get used to these pairs and groups of verbs being friends – then when you know one, you'll remember the other more easily. The words in bold rhyme.

	faire – to do	aller – to go
Je	**fais**	**vais**
Tu	fais	vas
Il	fait	va
Nous	faisons	allons
Vous	faites	allez
Ils	**font**	**vont**

	devoir – to have to	boire – to drink	recevoir – to receive
Je	**dois**	**bois**	**reçois**
Tu	**dois**	**bois**	**reçois**
Il	**doit**	**boit**	**reçoit**
Nous	devons	buvons	recevons
Vous	devez	buvez	recevez
Ils	**doivent**	**boivent**	**reçoivent**

	vouloir – to want	pouvoir to be able to
Je	**veux**	**peux**
Tu	**veux**	**peux**
Il	**veut**	**peut**
Nous	voulons	pouvons
Vous	voulez	pouvez
Ils	veulent	peuvent

More irregular verbs

1 **jeter / appeler** throw / call	2 **de- / venir / tenir** (be)come / hold	3 **com- / ap- /prendre** understand /learn / take
je jette / j'appelle tu jettes / appelles il jette / appelle nous jetons / appelons vous jetez / appelez ils jettent / appellent	je viens tu viens il vient nous venons vous venez ils viennent	je prends tu prends il prend nous prenons vous prenez ils prennent
4 **acheter, se lever** buy, get up	5 **voir / croire** see / believe	6 **sortir / partir /dormir** go out / leave / sleep
j'achète tu achètes il achète nous achetons vous achetez ils achètent	je vois / crois tu vois / crois il voit / croit voyons / croyons vous voyez / croyez ils voient / croient	pars / sors / dors pars / sors / dors part / sort / dort partons / sortons partez / sortez partent / sortent
7 **dire / lire / conduire** say / read / drive	8 **mettre / permettre** put / permit	9 **(d)écrire** write (describe)
je dis / lis / conduis tu dis / lis / conduis il dit / lit / / conduit disons/lisons/conduisons dites / lisez / conduisez disent/ lisent/conduisent	je mets tu mets il met nous mettons vous permettez ils permettent	j'écris tu écris il écrit nous écrivons vous écrivez ils écrivent

Group 1 – jeter, appeler, rappeler, projeter etc
These take a double consonant in all forms (persons 1,2,3,6) except *nous* and *vous* (persons 4 and5). Other examples of the 1236 format are the *devoir* group and the *vouloir* group above.

Group 2 – venir, revenir, devenir
These follow a pattern along the lines of 1236 above but with the extra i before the e in those forms of the verb, which disappears in *nous* and *vous*. 1236 have the i but 4 and 5 do not. Note the double n in 3rd person plural as well. I remember it as "*come to Vienna*".

Group 3 – prendre, comprendre, apprendre
With to *take*, you *take* out the d for the second half, and like *venir*, a double n in *the* ils form. Venir and prendre have rhyming last lines.

Group 4 – acheter, se lever
Here the 1236 relates to a grave accent which disappears in *nous* and *vous* forms. So 4 and 5 are accent-less.

Group 5 – voire, croire
Here the 1236 relates to an i which is replaced by a y in the *nous* and *vous* forms. It reminds me of *crayons* and *Croydon*.

Group 6 – partir, sortir, dormir
This is the teenager group - all teenagers do is go out, sleep, and leave. Where do they go out of? The doors (*dors*). Once you have the word *dors*, you have *pars* and *sors*, and the rest follows.

Group 7 – conduire, lire, dire, construire, détruire, réduire
The single s in forms 4,5,6 sounds like a z, and could be the noise of the *car engine* (you're *driving*, the passenger is *saying* things, car is *producing* gases that we must *reduce* because they *destroy* clean air).

Group 8 – mettre, permettre, promettre
Start with *je mets la table* and the rest should follow.

Group 9 – écrire, décrire
This may sound rather far-fetched, but if you write something which is *right*, you get a *tick*. A tick is shaped like a v, hence the v in the plural of écrire. *Nous écrivons, vous écrivez, ils écrivent.*

Faire and aller – with activities

If it's a **game** that you can win use **jouer au** (**aux** for plural)

Je joue au tennis
Je joue au netball
Je joue au basket
Je joue aux cartes / aux échecs / aux jeux-vidéo

With **instruments** it's **jouer du or de la**

Je joue du piano   (« du du du » goes the piano)
Je joue de la guitare   (« la la la » singing to the guitar)

Use **faire du** with masculine activities: Je fais…

du sport	sport
du vélo / VTT	cycling
du patinage	skating
du ski	skiing
du jogging	jogging

Use **faire de la** if it's feminine (mostly in the **sea**): Je fais…

de la natation	swimming
de la voile	sailing
de la planche à voile	windsurfing
de la plongée	diving
de la gymnastique	gymnastics (on the beach!)
de la danse	dance (also on the beach!)

If it begins with a **vowel** use **faire de l'**

Je fais de l'équitation   I go horseriding
Il fait de l'athlétisme   He does athletics

If you do lots of them, like walks, **faire des**

Elle fait des promenades   She goes for walks
On a fait des randonnées   We went hiking

The past tense (passé composé)

To form this, tense, which is used to talk about past events, use the person, auxiliary and past participle.

The person is the subject of the verb and can be a person's name or a pronoun that represents it.

The auxiliary is the present tense of avoir or être.

The past participle is formed like this: *Verbs ending in -er go to é*
Verbs ending in -re go to u
Verbs ending in -ir go to i

Examples

Ils ont **joué** au foot	They played football
Nous avons **ecouté** le prof	We listened to the teacher
Mon père a **vendu** la maison	My father sold the house
J'ai **entendu** le bruit	I heard the noise
Sandrine a **choisi** ses amis	Sandrine chose her friends
Je suis **allé** à la banque	I went to the bank
Jean est **arrivé** à midi	Jean arrived at midday.

Most verbs take the auxiliary avoir in the past tense but a certain number take être. (See the last two examples above.)

So how do we know which auxiliary to use? Some schools teach *Dr/Mrs Vandertramp* as a mnemonic for this list, and there are some reasons to use it, for example you can quickly establish that a verb like *quitter* does not take être because there is no Q in the mnemonic at all, but if you are given a verb like *rester* or *ranger*, how do you establish quickly whether or not it is one of the Rs in the mnemonic? This is why I prefer the image of the house on the next page. When you are having to conjugate a verb in the past tense, just picture this house and ask yourself: Is that verb in the house?

Verbs that take être (house verbs and bedroom verbs)

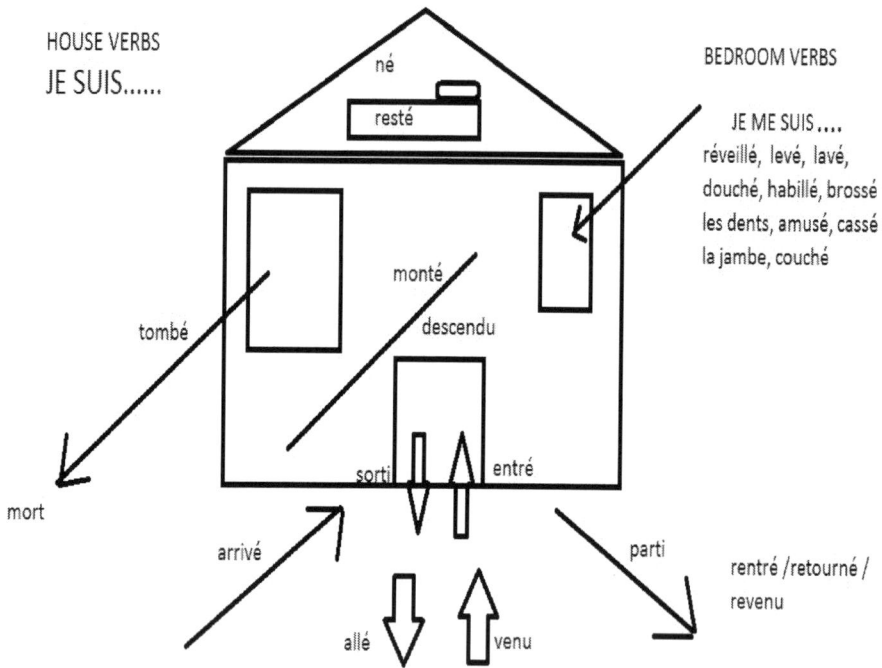

HOUSE VERBS

JE SUIS......

né

resté

monté

descendu

tombé

mort

sorti

entré

arrivé

parti

allé

venu

BEDROOM VERBS

JE ME SUIS ....
réveillé, levé, lavé,
douché, habillé, brossé
les dents, amusé, cassé
la jambe, couché

rentré /retourné /
revenu

The difference between these verbs and the ones that take **avoir** is that with these, *the past participle must agree* with the subject of the verb (the person that did it) in gender and number. Add *e* for feminine and *s* for plural. For example:

elle est tombée	she fell
nous sommes arrivées	we (fem plural) arrived
ils sont partis	they left (masc plural)
vous êtes sortis	you (masc plural) went out
nous sommes allés	we (masc plural) went

Irregular past participles

Here are the main ones:

avoir	→ J'ai eu	I had
boire	→ J'ai bu	I drank
croire	→ J'ai cru	I believed
devoir -	→ J'ai dû	I had to
savoir	→ J'ai su	I knew (fact)
voir	→ J'ai vu	I saw
pouvoir	→ J'ai pu	I was able to
connaître	→ J'ai connu	I knew (person)
lire	→ J'ai lu	I read
pleuvoir	→ Il a plu	It rained
venir	→ Je suis venu	I came
vouloir	→ J'ai voulu	I wanted
courir	→ J'ai couru	I ran
recevoir	→ J'ai reçu	I received
vivre	→ J'ai vécu	I lived
prendre	→ J'ai pris	I took
apprendre	→ J'ai appris	I learnt
comprendre	→ J'ai compris	I understood
mettre	→ J'ai mis	I put
dire	→ J'ai dit	I said
écrire	→ J'ai écrit	I wrote
conduire	→ J'ai conduit	I drove
construire	→ J'ai construit	I built
ouvrir	→ J'ai ouvert	I opened
faire	→ J'ai fait	I did / made
être	→ J'ai été	I was
naitre	→ Je suis né	I was born
mourir	→ il est mort	he died

The imperfect tense

- Use it for a repeated action in the past that you *used* to do.
  Quand *j'étais* jeune *je faisais* de la natation tous les jours.
  When *I was* young *I went swimming* every day.

- Use it to say "it was" (c'était) and "there was" (il y avait)

- Use **with the conditional** tense as we do in English.
  Si j'*étais* riche, j'achèterais un bateau.
  If *I was* rich, I would buy a boat.

- Use it when you are stressing the fact that this **WAS going on** rather than the completion of the action.
  Je nettoyais la maison quand il est arrivé.
  I was cleaning the house when he arrived.

- or to say **"was going to"** as in English
  J'allais faire mes devoirs, mais j'étais trop fatigué.
  I was going to do my homework but I was too tired.

To make and use the imperfect tense...
Take the nous form of the present tense (eg **jouons**), take the *ons* off and add the endings:

je jou**ais**	I played
tu jou**ais**	you played
il jou**ait**	he played
nous jou**ions**	we played
vous jou**iez**	you played
ils / elles jou**aient**	they played

The only exception is être – where you add the above endings on to *ét* because there is no *ons* to take off in the *nous* form.

The near future tense

In English we say, "I am going to eat an apple". We can translate this directly into French: **Je vais manger une pomme** = I am going to eat an apple. Use the present of **aller** + **infinitive**

Je vais
Tu vas
Il va   regarder / aller / sortir / faire / finir / répondre
Nous allons
Vous allez
Ils vont

Simple future tense (not so simple!)

This form of the future is made by putting special endings onto (usually) the infinitive. The endings come from the verb avoir.

manger	répondre	finir
je manger**ai** – I will eat	je répondr**ai**	je finir**ai**
tu manger**as** – you will eat	tu répondr**as**	tu finir**as**
il manger**a** – he will eat	il répondr**a**	il finir**a**
nous manger**ons** – we will eat	nous répondr**ons**	nous finir**ons**
vous manger**ez** – you will eat	vous répondr**ez**	vous finir**ez**
ils manger**ont** – they will eat	ils répondr**ont**	ils finir**ont**

The most important irregular future roots

avoir (to have)	j'**aur**ai	I will have
savoir (to know)	je **saur**ai	I will know
être (to be)	je **ser**ai	I will be
faire (to do)	je **fer**ai	I will do
aller (to go)	j'**ir**ai	I will go
pouvoir (be able)	je **pourr**ai	I will be able to
devoir (to have to)	je **devr**ai	I will have to
voir (to see)	je **verr**ai	I will see
venir (to come)	je **viendr**ai	I will come
vouloir (to want)	je **voudr**ai	I will want

The conditional tense

"If I **had** time.................... I **would play** tennis"
imperfect   conditional

Formation

To form the conditional, take the future stem (usually the infinitive) and add the imperfect endings:

manger	**répondre**	**finir**
je manger**ais**	je répondr**ais**	je finir**ais**
tu manger**ais**	tu répondr**ais**	tu finir**ais**
il manger**ait**	il répondr**ait**	il finir**ait**
nous manger**ions**	nous répondr**ions**	nous finir**ions**
vous manger**iez**	vous répondr**iez**	vous finir**iez**
ils manger**aient**	ils répondr**aient**	ils finir**aient**

But the same list of irregular future stems (ser, aur, ir, fer etc) applies as for the future tense.

Tu irais	You would go
Elle serait	She would be
Vous auriez	You would have
On ferait	We would do
Je saurais	I would know
Il pourrait	He would be able to (he could)
On devrait	We would have to (we should)

Si j'étais riche, j'achèterais un bateau.
If I was rich, I would buy a boat.

S'il y avait plus de pistes cyclables, je serais plus content.
If there were more cycle paths, I would be happier.

Si les profs donnaient moins de devoirs, je ferais plus de sport.
If the teachers gave us less homework, I would do more sport.

Si je pouvais changer quelque chose, je construirais une piscine.
If I could change something, I would build a swimming pool.

Summary of tenses and how to recognise them

Present (but be aware of irregulars)

-e –es –e ons ez ent

-s –s –d ons ez ent

-is –is –it issons issez issent

Passé composé

Person, auxiliary (avoir or être) and past participle (mostly in é, u or i). Watch out for irregular past participles (bu, lu, pu, vu, voulu, fait, pris etc) and remember to agree them after être (house) verbs.

Imperfect

Take the nous form, take the ons off, add the endings: **-ais – ais –ait –ions –iez –aient** (use ét as the root for être)

Near future

Present tense of aller plus infinitive – easy!

Simple future (not so simple)

Add the endings that look like avoir **-ai -as -a -ons -ez -ont** on the end of the infinitive OR on the end of a special future stem: *ser, aur, ir, fer, devr, pourr, enverr, verr, viendr, voudr, mourr, saur.*

Conditional

Future stem plus imperfect ending – the conditional has nothing of its own – it borrows from the future and the imperfect, and usually needs to be paired with an imperfect in the *if* sentence.

The subjunctive mood

Although this isn't strictly a tense, it's a form of the verb that the French use all the time and using it in your speaking and writing can really earn you points. It is used after *que* in expressions relating to importance, purpose, negative thinking, emotion and wanting someone to do something.

How to form the subjunctive

To form, the general rule is that you take the 3rd person plural of the present tense, remove *ent* and add: -e -es -e -ions -iez -ent

Que je prenne	from *prendre*
Que tu viennes	from *venir*
Qu'elle finisse	from *finir*
Qu'il joue	from *jouer*

Irregular subjunctives include

être – je sois	avoir – j'aie
aller – j'aille	faire – je fasse
pouvoir – je puisse	savoir – je sache

Use it with expressions concerning the importance / necessity of someone else doing something

Il faut que tu fasses des efforts.
You've got to make an effort.

Il faut que le gouvernement agisse.
The government must act.

Il faut que nous soyons prudents.
We've got to be careful.

Il faut qu'il prenne ses comprimés.
He must take his pills.

BUT Use *il faut* with an infinitive to express *general* importance

Il faut porter un uniforme.
We have to wear a uniform.

Il faut respecter les profs.
You have to respect the teachers.

Use it after negative thinking

Je ne pense pas que ce soit une bonne idée.
I don't think it's a good idea.

Je doute qu'il ait fini.
I doubt he has finished.

Use it with emotions

Je suis heureux qu'il soit là.
I'm happy that he's there.

Je suis ravi que tu sois venu.
I am delighted that you came.

Use it to express what people want others to do

Ma mère veut que je fasse mes devoirs.
My mother wants me to do my homework.

Il veut que je prenne le bus.
He wants me to take the bus

Use it to express purpose with *bien que* and *pour que*

On doit protéger l'environnement, bien que ce soit difficile, pour que nos enfants puissent survivre.
We must protect the environment, although it's difficult so that our children can survive.

J'achèterai une énorme maison, bien que ce soit cher, pour que mes amis puissent me rendre visite.
I will buy an enormous house, although it's expensive, so that my friends can visit me.

Il faut sensibiliser les jeunes aux dangers du tabac pour qu'ils sachent la vérité.

We must make young people aware of the dangers of tobacco so that they know the truth.

Quand je serai adulte, je vais continuer à faire du sport, bien que ce soit fatigant, pour que je puisse rester en forme.

When I'm older I'll carry on doing sport, although it's tiring, so that I can stay in shape.

PART 2

Speaking

The speaking exam is the one where you can get a long way through rote learning of prepared speeches and answers, but beware... You will also need to understand the questions, and with most exam boards take part in a role play where you will need to respond to instructions and ask your own questions.

Discussion - understanding questions

The first skill to master in your preparation for the oral exam is understanding the questions you are asked. The same question can be asked in a number of different ways. For example:

Quels sont tes passetemps préférés ?
What are your favourite hobbies?

Qu'est-ce que tu aimes faire pendant ton temps libre ?
What do you like to do in your free time?

Que fais-tu normalement pour t'amuser ?
What do you usually do to have fun?

Test yourself on the structures below to make sure you are ready for all forms of question before practising your answers.

Quel est …..?	Which is / What is…?
Quels sont…? / Quelles sont….?	Which are / What are…?
Que (eg que manges-tu?)	What (what are you eatting?)
A quelle heure ?	When (at what time?)
Quand ?	When (generally)?
Comment ?	How?
Comment est…?	What is …… like?
Où ?	Where?
Qui ?	Who?
Pourquoi ?	Why?
Décris / décrivez	Describe
Explique / expliquez	Explain
Raconte / racontez	Tell

Your presentation or prepared speech

Depending on your exam board, you may have to either describe a photo you have found yourself, (Edexcel IGCSE) answer questions on a photocard with a few minutes preparation time (AQA or Edexcel GCSE) or make a speech lasting about a minute on one of the set topics (Cambridge IGCSE). This seems unfair on those taking AQA or Edexcel GCSE but they have their chance to shine as they get to begin their general conversation with a one-minute prepared speech later on.

In the case of the prepared speeches, whether a picture or not, you should make sure you maximize your use of impressive phrases, use all the tenses you can cram in, and leave the examiner to ask boring questions like "what is he / she wearing?"

Here is an example of a description of a picture: this happens to be a cartoon picture of a family on a beach holiday, with a sinister shark fin poking out of the water. This would be an Edexcel IGCSE full marks answer:

Les vacances

Cette photo a été prise l'année dernière quand nous étions en vacances en Australie. Vous me voyez à gauche, allongée sur une serviette verte, vêtue de bikini, pendant que ma cousine est en train de construire un château de sable. A côté de moi il y a des parasols que l'on peut utiliser pour s'abriter de la chaleur. Tout près, mon père vient de prendre une photo de mon frère qui fait du surf. Il est plus courageux que moi et ma mère semble fière de lui car elle le regarde en souriant. Mais elle veut qu'il fasse attention !

Malheureusement personne n'a aperçu l'aileron du requin qui est sur le point de dévorer la moitié de ma famille. Quel cauchemar ! A l'arrière-plan un jeune homme fait du parapente et lui, comme le pilote du petit avion, aurait eu une vue magnifique de l'attaque de requin. Nous avons tous eu de la chance car il s'est avéré que le requin n'avait pas faim. A part ce presqu'accident, c'étaient des vacances parfaites, un petit coin de paradis et j'ai hâte d'y retourner un jour.

Translation

This photo was taken last year when we were on holiday in Australia. You can see me on the left, lying on a green towel, wearing a bikini, while my cousin is in the middle of building a sandcastle. Next to me there are parasols you can use to shelter from the heat. Near me, my father has just taken a photo of my brother who is surfing. He is braver than me and my mother seems proud of him as she is looking at him with a smile. But she wants him to be careful! Unfortunately, nobody has noticed the fin of the shark which is about to devour half my family. What a nightmare! In the background, a young man is parasailing, and he, like the pilot of the small plane, would have had a magnificent view of the shark attack. We were all lucky as it turned out the shark wasn't hungry. Apart from this near miss, this was a perfect holiday in a little corner of paradise, and I can't wait to go back there one day.

Basic follow-up questions

After talking about a photo, you can expect a specific question relating to a particular person in it : **Que fait-il ? / Que fait-elle ?**

> Mon petit cousin qu'on voit au premier plan n'a pas encore appris à nager donc il est sur le point d'aller dans la mer avec une bouée mais il a été distrait par un crabe géant qui se précipite vers le château de sable.
>
> *My little cousin who you can see in the foreground has not yet learnt to swim so he's about to go in the sea with a rubber ring, but he has been distracted by a giant crab which is hurrying towards the sand castle.*

Next, they may ask you about the weather, and some specific questions about various people in the picture, what they are wearing, doing, or saying. Make sure you know the words for all the clothes items and accessories in the picture, and practise them with the colours, making sure to agree the colour with the gender and number of the item eg. *elle porte une chemise verte.*

Complex follow-up questions

This will be followed by questions on what happened before the photo (inviting you to use the past tense), what's going to happen next (inviting the future tense, and questions involving the word *ideal* (inviting the conditional tense).

PAST: Qu'est-ce qui s'est passé avant la photo ?

Be prepared to describe what happened before the photo – taking each person in turn, so you need to know your past tense verbs in the he and the they form:

Sample answer – relating to you

> Je me suis réveillé je me suis levé, je suis descendu, j'ai pris mon petit déjeuner. J'ai pris un croissant, un jus d'orange et des fraises, et après avoir mangé j'ai décidé d'aller à la plage parce qu'il faisait beau et j'avais envie de me bronzer.
>
> *I woke up, got up, went downstairs, had my breakfast. I had a croissant, an orange juice and strawberries, and after having eaten I decided to go to the beach and I felt like sunbathing.*

Alternative answers relating to other people in the picture

> **Il / elle** s'est réveillé(e) / s'est levé(e) / est descendu(e) / a pris son petit déjeuner et après avoir mangé il / elle a décidé d'aller à la plage car il / elle avait envie de se bronzer.
>
> **Ils** se sont réveillé(e)s / sont descendu(e)s / ont pris leur petit déjeuner, ont décidé d'aller à la plage car ils / elles avaient envie de se bronzer.

FUTURE : Après la photo

Here you will need your future tense verbs as they relate to you and the others in the picture.

Sample answer – relating to you

> Après avoir passé la journée à la plage, je vais retourner à l'hôtel pour prendre une douche. Je ferai une petite sieste avant de descendre au restaurant pour manger.

Après avoir mangé je vais sortir en boite sans que mes parents ne le sachent et je vais rentrer avant qu'ils se réveillent le lendemain, donc ils n'en sauront rien !

After having spent the day at the beach, I will go back to the hotel to take a shower. I will have a little nap before going down to the restaurant to eat. After eating I will go clubbing without my parents knowing and I will get back before they wake up the next day, so they won't know anything about it!

Alternative answer relating to other people in the picture

Après avoir passé la journée à la plage, il va retourner à l'hôtel pour prendre une douche. Il fera une petite sieste avant de descendre au restaurant pour manger. Après avoir mangé, il va sortir en boite sans que ses parents ne le sachent et il va rentrer avant qu'ils se réveillent le lendemain, donc ils n'en sauront rien !

After having spent the day at the beach, he will go back to the hotel to take a shower. He will have a little nap before going down to the restaurant to eat. After eating he will go clubbing without his parents knowing and he will get back before they wake up the next day, so they won't know anything about it!

CONDITIONAL : les vacances idéales

Here you will need the conditional tense, but start with the imperfect so that you have a nice "if" sentence to start it all off – another box ticked!

Sample answer

Si j'étais riche, j'irais en Espagne mais avec mes amis au lieu de ma famille. On resterait dans un hôtel de luxe près de la plage. J'y irais en avion, première classe, et j'irais à l'hôtel en limousine. Il y aurait tout ce dont j'ai besoin, une piscine, un cinéma, et des courts de tennis réservés pour moi, à l'ombre bien sûr pour éviter la chaleur.

If I was rich I'd go to Spain but with my friends instead of my family. We'd stay in a luxury hotel near the beach. I'd go by plane first class and I'd go to the hotel in a limousine. There would be everything I needed, a pool, a cinema, and tennis courts reserved for me in the shade of course to avoid the heat.

Unseen photo description (for AQA and Edexcel GCSE)

There are a few tactics you can adopt here. Say who is in the picture, where they are, what they are doing (en train de = in the middle of) and how they are feeling. Chances are, there will be close-ups of people, at least one of whom is smiling. Try this:

Sur la photo il y a trois personnes – deux femmes et un homme. Ils sont en train de trier les déchets dans la cuisine avant de les mettre dans les boites de recyclage. Je pense que les femmes sont contentes car elles sourient.

In the photo there are three people – two women and one man. They are in the middle of sorting out the rubbish in the kitchen before putting it into the recycling bins. I think the women are happy because they are smiling.

Use your preparation time not only to get your answers ready to the given questions but to think what kind of surprise questions might follow. These questions will be on the same theme as your picture but are likely to be on another topic within that theme. Remind yourself of those topics so you're ready to talk about them. Depending on your board, you may be allowed to take notes in to help you with the picture and role play task. Make sure you do that, even if you don't think you need to, just in case you panic once in the exam room.

Top tips for the conversation

- **The examiner wants you to succeed** – so don't imagine that they are trying to trip you up. It is likely to be your own teacher testing you and he or she will want you to get the best result possible.

- **Listen for key words** such as

  idéal (inviting the conditional)

  jeune (when you were younger, so imperfect)

  Le week-end dernier (inviting passe compose)

  Le week-end prochain (inviting future)

  changer (what you'd like to change, so begin by saying what you don't like)

  tu préfères (you will need to compare two things)

  NB The way to pronounce préfère (as in *I prefer*) is to say it exactly like you do in English. This avoids it sounding like the French for *favourite* which is *préféré*)

- **They are looking to tick boxes.** The recording will be sent off to moderators and needs to show your mastery of all the main tenses and a good knowledge of the language overall. So if you keep getting asked the same type of question, then chances are you have not yet successfully demonstrated your knowledge of a particular tense.

- **Keep talking!** Stay on topic, but the more you speak the fewer questions will be asked, and the longer you are in control.

- **Take your time** before answering and remember you can ask the examiner to repeat a question. *(Répétez la question s'il vous plait)*

- **Don't panic**. It will be over in a few minutes. Smile, breathe and enjoy!

WHERE YOU LIVE

Describe your town

J'habite à Wimbledon dans le sud-ouest de Londres, près de Kingston. C'est une ville moderne avec des endroits historiques. J'ai de la chance parce qu'à mon avis c'est la meilleure région de Londres et j'y habite depuis ma naissance. Ce que j'aime c'est qu'il y a tout ce dont j'ai besoin et je ne m'ennuie jamais. On peut aller au cinéma, faire du shopping ou jouer au tennis au parc. Mais, ce que je n'aime pas c'est la circulation – parfois il me faut une demie-heure pour aller en ville en bus. S'il y avait plus de pistes cyclables j'irais à vélo mais il n'y en a pas assez donc c'est trop dangereux.

I live in Wimbledon in south-west London near Kingston. It's a modern town with some older parts. I'm lucky because in my opinion it's the best part of London and I've lived there since I was born. What I like is that there is everything I need, and I never get bored. You can go to the cinema, go shopping or play tennis in the park; but what I don't like is the traffic. Sometimes it takes me half an hour to get into town on the bus. If there were more cycle paths, I'd go by bike but there aren't enough so it's too dangerous.

Describe a recent activity in your town

Le week-end dernier je suis allé en ville avec ma sœur pour acheter un cadeau pour l'anniversaire de ma mère. Je lui ai acheté un livre car elle adore la lecture. Après ça, nous sommes allés au cinéma pour regarder un film de James Bond, que j'ai beaucoup aimé car il y avait de bons effets spéciaux. Ensuite, nous sommes allés au café pour manger un sandwich. Après avoir mangé, nous sommes rentrés chez nous en bus.

Last weekend I went into town with my sister to buy a present for my mother's birthday. I bought her a book as she loves reading. After that we went to the cinema to see a James Bond film which I loved because there were great special effects. Then we went to the café for a sandwich. After eating we went home by bus.

What is there for young people in your town?

Il n'y a pas grand-chose pour les jeunes, il faut l'admettre. On peut aller au cinéma ou à la piscine, on peut faire du shopping ou du bowling, mais tout ça coute cher et la plupart des jeunes n'ont pas les moyens. Ce qu'il manque c'est un endroit où on peut retrouver ses amis quand il fait mauvais, comme un club de jeunesse. S'il y en avait un, nous serions tous ravis. A part ça, je pense qu'il devrait y avoir plus de pistes cyclables pour qu'on puisse aller partout à vélo. Ainsi, on pourrait non seulement rester en forme mais aussi réduire la pollution de l'air et protéger l'environnement.

There isn't much for young people I must admit. You can go to the cinema or the pool, go shopping or bowling but all that costs money and most young people can't afford it. What's missing is a place you can meet up with friends when the weather is bad like a youth club. If there was one we would all be so happy. Apart from that I think there should be more cycle paths so we can go everywhere by bike. That way we could not only keep fit but reduce air pollution and protect the environment.

What would you do to improve your town?

Si j'avais l'occasion d'améliorer ma ville, je ferais quelque chose pour les jeunes, parce qu'il n'y a pas grand-chose en ce moment. On peut aller au cinéma ou à la piscine, on peut faire du shopping ou du bowling, mais tout ça coute cher et la plupart des jeunes n'ont pas les moyens. Ce qu'il manque c'est un endroit où on peut retrouver ses amis quand il fait mauvais, comme un club de jeunesse. S'il y en avait un, nous serious tous ravis. A part ça, je pense qu'il devrait y avoir plus de pistes cyclables pour qu'on puisse aller partout à vélo. Ainsi, on pourrait non seulement rester en forme mais aussi réduire la pollution de l'air et protéger l'environnement.

If I had the chance to improve my town, I would do something for the young people. You can go to the cinema or the pool, go shopping or bowling but all that costs money and most young people can't afford it. What's missing is a place you can meet up with friends when the weather is bad like a youth club. If there was one, we would all be so happy. Apart from that I think there should be more cycle paths so we can go everywhere by bike. That way we could not only keep fit but reduce air pollution and protect the environment.

What is there for tourists in your town?

Pour les touristes, on est super-bien situé pour aller au championnat de tennis, et on peut facilement aller à Londres en train pour visiter les sites touristiques comme le palais de Buckingham et la Tour de Londres, aussi bien que les musées et les galléries d'art. Au centre de Londres il y a plein de théâtres où on peut voir des spectacles mondialement célèbres, mais les billets coutent les yeux de la tête.

For the tourists, we are perfectly placed for the tennis championships and you can get to London easily by train to see the tourist attractions like Buckingham Palace and the Tower of London as well as the museums and art galleries. In the centre of London there are lots o theatres where you can see world famous shows, but the tickets cost an arm and a leg.

Advantages of living in a town

L'avantage d'habiter en ville c'est qu'il y a tout ce dont j'ai besoin et plein de choses à faire. En plus je peux facilement retrouver mes amis en utilisant les transports en commun. Je trouve les bus indispensables. Je m'en sers tous les jours et je ne pourrais pas m'en passer.

The advantage of living in town is that there is everything I need and lots of things to do. Also, I can easily meet up with my friends using public transport. I find the buses essential. I use them every day and couldn't manage without them.

Disadvantages of living in a town

Ce que je n'aime pas tellement c'est la pollution de l'air causée par les gaz d'échappement. La pollution provoque le réchauffement de la terre et l'effet de serre mais il me semble que les gens sont trop égoïstes pour abandonner le confort de leurs voitures et prendre le bus. En plus, il n'y a pas assez de pistes cyclables. S'il y en avait plus, j'irais partout à vélo.

What I don't like so much is the air pollution caused by car emissions. Pollution causes global warming and the greenhouse effect, but it seems that people are too selfish to abandon the comfort of their cars and take the bus. Also, there aren't enough cycle paths. If there were more, I'd go everywhere by bike.

Advantages of the countryside
A la campagne c'est moins pollué qu'en ville et il y a plus d'espaces verts où on peut se promener et respirer l'air frais. Les prix immobiliers sont plus bas car le terrain coute moins cher. Il y a beaucoup moins de circulation, donc on peut faire du vélo sans avoir peur d'être écrasé par un bus.

In the countryside it's less polluted than in the town and there are more green spaces where you can walk and breathe fresh air. The house prices are lower as land is cheaper. There is a lot less traffic so you can cycle without worrying about being run over by a bus.

Disadvantages of the countryside
A la campagne, bien que ce soit plus tranquille et plus calme, il n'y a pas grand-chose à faire et on doit aller partout en voiture car il n'y a pas de transports en commun. Je ne voudrais jamais y habiter car je me sentirais trop isolé.

In the countryside, although it's quieter and calmer, there isn't much to do and you ha,ve to go everywhere by car as there is no public transport. I would never want to live there as I'd feel too isolated.

Weather in your region today
Aujourd'hui il fait assez beau mais le ciel est couvert et il va pleuvoir des grenouilles, j'en suis sûr.

Today the weather is quite good but it's cloudy and it's going to pour with rain I'm sure.

Seasonal changes

Normalement en hiver il fait un froid de canard, en été il fait chaud, et au printemps et en automne c'est entre les deux. Du coup, en hiver je fais moins de sport, et je joue au tennis à l'intérieur quand il pleut. Par contre, en été je suis dehors tous les jours. Je passe tout mon temps libre à jouer au tennis et à faire du vélo, car ça fait du bien d'être en plein air et c'est bon pour la santé.

Normally in winter it's freezing cold, in summer it's hot and in the spring and autumn it's between the two. So, in winter I do less sport and I play tennis indoors when it's raining. But in summer I'm outside every day. I spend all my free time playing tennis and going cycling, because it feels good to be out in the fresh air and it's good for you.

Climate comparison – England and France

Il n'y a pas beaucoup de différence entre le climat en Angleterre et en France. Mais au sud de la France il fait plus chaud qu'en Angleterre. Plus on va vers le sud, plus la température augmente. C'est le contraire au nord de l'Angleterre – plus on va vers le nord, plus le temps s'empire.

There isn't much difference between the climate in England and France. But in the south of France it's hotter than in England. The further you go southwards, the hotter it gets. It's the opposite in the north of England – the further north you go, the worse the weather gets.

Transport in your region

Puisque j'habite à Londres, il y a tous les moyens de transport dont on pourrait avoir besoin – et comme c'est une très grande ville c'est bien de pouvoir se déplacer facilement. On peut prendre le bus, le train, le métro, le tramway et les vélos municipaux qui se trouvent partout. Il suffit de s'enregistrer et on peut prendre un vélo et le déposer ailleurs. Moi je m'en sers tous les jours, pour aller au collège, chez des amis, en ville, quoi que ce soit.

Since I live in London, there are all the modes of transport you could possibly need – and as it's a very big city it's good to be able to move around easily. You can take the bus, train, underground, tram and community bikes which are everywhere. You just have to register and you can take a bike and drop it off elsewhere. I use them every day to go to school to friends' houses, into town, whatever.

Favourite transport

Mon moyen de transport préféré c'est le bus, parce que je m'installe en avant, en haut, et je vois tout qui se passe autour de moi. En plus j'adore faire du vélo. Ce que je n'aime pas, pourtant, c'est le manque de pistes cyclables. On devrait en construire plus pour que les gens puissent se déplacer sans causer la pollution de l'air. Je suis accro au cyclisme et je trouve que c'est un passe-temps dangereux en ville.

My favourite mode of transport is the bus because I sit at the front on top and I see everything that's going on around me. I also love cycling. What I don't like however is the lack of cycle paths. We need to build more so that people can get around without causing air pollution. I'm a cycling addict and I find that it's a dangerous hobby in town.

HOLIDAYS AND FESTIVALS

French-speaking countries you've been to

Je suis allé en France plusieurs fois et je l'ai beaucoup aimée, car le paysage est pittoresque et la cuisine est la meilleure du monde. En plus, le climat est plus agréable qu'en Angleterre. Quant aux autres pays francophones, j'en connais, mais je ne les ai pas visités. On parle français aux îles Caraïbes et en Afrique du nord, mais je n'y suis jamais allé.

I've been to France many times and I liked it a lot, as the scenery is picturesque and the food is the best in the world. Also, the weather is better than in England. As for other French speaking countries, I know some, but I haven't been to any. They speak French in the Caribbean and in North Africa, but I've never been there.

Usual holidays

J'ai de la chance car nous passons la plupart des vacances en Espagne. J'y vais chaque année en avion avec ma famille. Il y a beaucoup de choses à faire, comme la natation, l'équitation, et la voile. Moi, je passe tout mon temps à jouer au tennis. J'y joue tout le temps, j'y suis accro, je ne pourrais pas m'en passer. J'aime l'Espagne parce qu'il fait beau tout le temps et ne pleut que rarement.

I'm lucky because we spend most of the holidays in Spain. I go there every year by plane with my family. There are lots of things to do like swimming, horse-riding and sailing. I spend all my time playing tennis. I play it all the time, I'm addicted, I couldn't manage without it. I like Spain because the weather is good all the time and it only rarely rains.

Last year's holiday

L'année dernière je suis allé en France en avion avec mes parents. Nous sommes restés dans un hôtel de cinq étoiles au bord de la mer. On a eu de la chance car il faisait beau tous les jours, donc on a pu passer la plupart du temps en plein air. Nous sommes allés à la plage où j'ai appris à faire de la planche à voile et on a gouté les plats régionaux qui étaient délicieux. Nous avons visité des sites touristiques et j'ai pris des photos pour montrer à mes copains. C'était super-chouette. J'ai hâte d'y retourner.

Last year I went to France by plane with my parents. We stayed in a five-star hotel at the seaside. We were lucky because the weather was good every day, so we were able to spend most of the time in the fresh air. We went to the beach where I learnt to windsurf, and we tasted the local dishes which were delicious. We visited tourist attractions and I took pictures to show my friends. It was great. I can't wait to go back there.

Purchases on holiday

En Espagne j'ai acheté un t-shirt pour mon ami avec un taureau dessus parce que c'est l'animal national de l'Espagne. Il l'a adoré. Quand je suis allé en France j'ai rapporté du confit de canard car c'était le plat typique de la région et on ne peut pas le trouver dans les supermarchés anglais.

In Spain I bought a T-shirt for my friend with a bull on it because it's the national animal of Spain. He loved it. When I went to France, I brought back confit de canard because it was the local speciality and you can't find it in the English supermarkets.

Future holiday

Cette année j'irai en Italie avec ma famille en avion, pour quinze jours. Nous allons rester dans un hôtel près de la plage où on peut faire de la planche à voile et de la natation. J'en profiterai pour me détendre après mes examens car j'aurai besoin de repos. Je n'en ferai pas une rame. J'espère qu'il fera beau pour que je puisse passer tout mon temps dehors.

This year I'm going to go to Italy with my family by plane for a fortnight. We will stay in a hotel near the beach where you canl go windsurfing and swimming. I'll make the most of it to relax after my exams as I'll be in need of a rest. I won't lift a finger. I hope that the weather will be good so I can spend all my time outside.

Ideal holiday

Si j'étais riche, j'irais en Espagne mais avec mes amis au lieu de ma famille. On resterait dans un hôtel de luxe près de la plage. J'y irais en avion, première classe, et j'irais à l'hôtel en limousine. Je jouerais au tennis tous les jours avec les meilleurs entraineurs du monde pour que je puisse devenir champion du monde. Il y aurait tout ce dont j'ai besoin, une piscine, un cinéma, et des courts de tennis réservés pour moi, à l'ombre bien sûr pour éviter la chaleur.

If I was rich, I'd go to Spain but with my friends instead of my family. We'd stay in a luxury hotel near the beach. I'd go by plane first class and I'd go to the hotel in a limousine. I'd play tennis every day with the best trainers in the country so that I could become world champion. There would be everything I needed, a pool, a cinema, and tennis courts reserved for me in the shade of course to avoid the heat.

Holidays with parents v holidays with friends

Si on part en vacances avec les parents, c'est facile et c'est gratuit. Ils paient tout et on ne doit penser à rien. Cependant, c'est eux qui décident ce qui est permis, et on n'a pas beaucoup de choix. Ils me trainent aux musées les plus ennuyeux du monde et j'en ai marre. Avec les amis, on peut s'amuser beaucoup plus, on peut sortir quand on veut, rentrer quand on veut et manger ce qu'on veut. J'ai hâte de partir avec mes copains dès que j'aurai l'occasion.

If you go on holiday with parents, it's easy and free. They pay for everything and you don't need to think about anything. However, they are the ones that decide what is allowed and you don't get much choice. They drag me round the most boring museums in the world and I'm sick of it. With friends you can have much more fun, you can go out when you like, come back when you like and eat what you like. I can't wait to go away with my friends as soon as I get the chance.

Essential ingredients of a holiday

Pour moi ce qui est important c'est le climat. Il faut que le temps soit ensoleillé mais je n'aime pas une chaleur insupportable. En plus, j'aimerais avoir mes amis avec moi, car on s'amuse tellement bien ensemble. Aussi, il faut loger dans un hôtel de luxe pour pouvoir se détendre et oublier le stress de la vie à Londres.

For me what's important is the climate. The weather has to be sunny, but I don't like unbearable heat. Also, I'd like to have my friends with me, as we have so much fun together. And we'd have to be in a luxury hotel in order to be able to relax and forget the stress of London life.

Importance of holidays

Bien que j'adore ma maison et mon quartier, je trouve que les vacances sont essentielles pour beaucoup de raisons. On peut se détendre après avoir travaillé pendant des mois. On peut explorer de nouveaux pays et connaitre de nouvelles cultures. On peut essayer de nouvelles activités et gouter la cuisine régionale. Mais ce que je trouve le plus important c'est passer du temps avec ma famille, car normalement on ne se voit pas assez souvent.

Although I love my house and my area, I find that holidays are essential for many reasons. You can relax after working for months. You can explore new countries and get to know new cultures. You can try out new activities and taste the local dishes. But what I find most important is spending time with my family as normally we don't see each other often enough.

Camping

Je n'ai jamais fait de camping, mais j'ai envie de l'essayer car ça me parait super-amusant de vivre en plein air dans une tente.

Cependant, je ne voudrais pas tellement dormir parterre sans matelas. Ça doit faire mal, non?

I've never been camping but I'd like to try it as it seems really fun to live outdoors in a tent. However, I wouldn't really like to sleep on the floor without a mattress. That must hurt, surely!

Festivals in England

Il n'y a pas beaucoup de festivals en Angleterre. Le seul festival qu'on fête normalement chez moi c'est noël. J'adore noël, car j'ai l'occasion de passer du temps avec ma famille, y compris les cousins que je ne vois qu'une fois par an. On mange un repas splendide et après avoir regardé le discours de la reine à la télé, on joue aux jeux de société ensemble et on échange des cadeaux. Ça fait du bien, passer du temps en famille.

There aren't many festivals in England. The only one that we normally celebrate in my family is Christmas. I love Christmas as I have the chance to spend time with my family, including the cousins that I only see once a year. We eat an amazing meal and after watching the Queen's speech we play board games together and exchange presents. It feels good spending time with family.

Last Christmas

L'année dernière toute ma famille est venue chez nous, y compris mes cousins que je ne vois qu'une fois par an. On a mangé un repas splendide, et après avoir regardé le discours de la reine à la télé on a joué aux jeux de société ensemble et on a échangé des cadeaux. J'ai offert une peinture à ma grand-mère et elle en était ravie. Moi j'ai reçu des vêtements et des nouveaux baskets dont j'avais rêvé depuis longtemps. C'était super.

Last year all my family came to us including my cousins whom I only see once a year. We ate an amazing meal and after watching the Queen's speech we played board games together and exchanged presents. I gave a painting to my granny and she was delighted. I received clothes and new trainers I'd been dreaming about for ages. It was great.

Importance of festivals

Les festivals sont importants car on n'a pas souvent l'occasion de passer du temps en famille et ça fait du bien. En Angleterre c'est dommage parce qu'on accorde de moins en moins d'importance à la religion, et c'est en abandonnant la religion qu'on perd les fêtes. En Espagne par exemple, il y a la fête de Pâques qui dure une semaine tandis que chez moi ce n'est que deux jours fériés pleins de chocolat.

Festivals are important because we don't often get the chance to spend time together as a family and it feels good. In England it's a shame because religion has become less and less important and it's in abandoning religion that we lose our festivals. In Spain for example there is the festival of Easter that lasts a week whereas here it's just two bank holidays full of chocolate.

EDUCATION

Describe your school

Mon collège s'appelle …………… et se trouve à ……………….., près de Londres. J'ai de la chance parce que c'est le meilleur collège du monde et j'y vais depuis cinq ans. C'est un collège pour les garçons, c'est grand, ancien, et bien équipé. Il y a environ mille élèves. Il y a des salles de classe, des terrains de sport où on peut jouer au foot, des laboratoires, une bibliothèque et une cantine.

My school is called .... and it is in ....
near London. I'm lucky because it's the best school in the world and
I've been going there for five years. It's a boys' school, it's big, old
and well equipped. There are about a thousand students. There are
classrooms, sports fields where you can play football, laboratories,
a library and a canteen.

Likes and dislikes at school

Ce que j'aime c'est que j'ai beaucoup d'amis, les profs sont sympas
et on peut faire beaucoup de sport. Ce que je n'aime pas c'est que
les profs nous donnent trop de devoirs, on doit porter un uniforme et
les règles sont strictes – par exemple on ne peut pas parler en classe,
et on ne peut pas utiliser les portables.

What I like is that I have lots of friends, the teachers are nice and
you can do a lot of sport. What I don't like is that the teachers give
us too much homework. Also, we have to wear a uniform and the
rules are strict – for example we can't talk in class and we can't use
mobile phones.

The school day

La journée scolaire commence à huit heures et termine à quatre
heures. Je suis obligé de me lever à sept heures et demie pour que je
puisse arriver au collège à l'heure. J'ai de la chance car j'habite tout
près de mon collège, donc j'y vais à pied et parfois j'arrive de bonne
heure et j'en profite pour terminer mes devoirs et envoyer des textos.
Dès que j'arrive au collège, je retrouve mes amis et on bavarde avant
que les cours commencent à 9h. Il y a huit cours par jour et chaque
cours dure 45 minutes. La pause déjeuner est à 1h. Pendant la pause
je mange un sandwich et je joue au foot avec mes amis. Les cours
finissent à 4h et je rentre chez moi, mais je ne peux me relaxer
qu'après avoir fait mes devoirs.

My school day begins at 8am and finishes at 4pm. I have to get up at 7am so I can get to school on time. I'm lucky because I live very near my school, so I go there on foot and sometimes I get there early and make the most of it to finish my homework and send some texts. As soon as I arrive at school, I meet my friends and chat before lessons begin at 9. There are 8 lessons a day and each lesson lasts 45 minutes. The lunch hour is at 1. During the break I eat a sandwich and play football with my friends. Lessons finish at 4 and I go home but I can only relax when I've done my homework.

Favourite subjects

Ma matière préférée c'est le français parce que j'ai de bonnes notes, je le trouve facile et le prof est sympa. Je n'aime pas le latin parce que je le trouve ennuyeux, le prof est nul et il nous donne trop de devoirs. Aussi, j'étudie les maths, les sciences, l'anglais, le sport, le dessin, la musique, la géo et l'histoire.

My favourite subject is French because I get good marks, I find it easy and the teacher is nice. I don't like Latin because I find it boring, the teacher is rubbish and gives us too much homework. I also do maths, science, English, sport, art, music, geography and history.

Describe a teacher

Mon prof préféré c'est Monsieur Macpherson, mon prof d'histoire. Il est super-sympa et marrant et ne nous donne pas trop de devoirs. Cependant il est très intelligent et il n'y a rien qu'il ne sait pas. Je l'admire pour ça, car j'aimerais être aussi intelligent que lui.

My favourite teacher is Mr Macpherson my history teacher. He is really nice and funny and doesn't give too much homework. However, he is very clever and there's nothing he doesn't know. I admire him for that, as I'd like to be as clever as him.

Yesterday at school

Hier j'ai eu une journée parfaite. Je suis arrivé au collège à huit heures et après avoir mis mes affaires dans mon casier, j'ai pris mes cahiers et mes livres pour les deux premiers cours.

Puis je suis allé à ma salle de classe et j'ai bavardé avec mes amis. Le prof de maths a annulé notre contrôle et le prof d'anglais était absent. Pendant la pause déjeuner mes copains et moi sommes allés au terrain de sport pour jouer au foot. L'après-midi il n'y avait que deux cours de plus car j'ai dû participer au concours de tennis et heureusement j'ai gagné !

Yesterday I had a perfect day. I arrived at school at 8 and after putting my things in my locker I took my books for the first two lessons. Then I went to my classroom and chatted with my friends. The maths teacher cancelled our test and the English teacher was away. During lunch my friends and I went to the sports field to play football. In the afternoon there were only two more lessons as I had to play in the tennis competition and luckily I won!

Describe school uniform

A mon école on doit porter un uniforme. Je porte un pantalon noir, une chemise blanche, des chaussures noires, des chaussettes noires, une cravate et une veste.

At my school we have to wear a uniform. I wear black trousers, a white shirt, black shoes, black socks, a tie and a jacket.

Opinion of school uniform

Bien que l'uniforme soit utile pour encourager la discipline, je trouve qu'on ne peut pas montrer son individualité quand tout le monde se ressemble. J'aurais peut-être du mal au début si je devais penser à mes vêtements tous les jours, mais cela dit, j'aimerais mieux imiter le système français et m'habiller comme je veux.

Although uniform is useful to encourage discipline, I find that you can't show your individuality when everyone looks the same. I might find it hard at first if I had to think about my clothes every day but having said that, I would rather do as the French do and wear what I like.

Importance of homework

Normalement je fais mes devoirs dans la cuisine, mais hier soir j'ai dû faire mes devoirs de maths et de français dans ma chambre parce qu'on avait des invités. Je trouve les devoirs utiles pour pratiquer ce qu'on a appris en classe, mais si j'étais prof je ne les donnerais pas chaque semaine. Parfois on devrait avoir le droit de se détendre un peu.

Normally I do my homework in the kitchen but last night I had to do my French and maths homework in my bedroom because we had visitors. I find homework useful to practice what we have learnt in class, but if I was a teacher, I wouldn't give it every week. Sometimes we should be able to relax a bit.

Importance of rules

Il y a des règles qui sont importantes et des autres qui sont bêtes. Par exemple, on doit respecter les profs et faire les devoirs et ça je comprends, mais on ne peut pas utiliser les portables en classe, et ils sont tellement utiles pour prendre des photos du tableau et pour faire des recherches en ligne. De plus on est obligé de porter un uniforme, et c'est moche et démodé.

There are rules which are important and others which are stupid. For example, you have to respect the teachers and do homework and that I understand, but you can't use phones in class, and they are so useful to take photos of the board and to do research online. What's more, we have to wear a uniform and it's ugly and old-fashioned.

School trips

Hier, j'ai eu de la chance car moi et mes amis sommes allés à Londres pour assister à un concert. C'était un voyage scolaire avec tous mes copains qui étudient la musique. La musique était extraordinaire et je l'ai adorée. Je suis rentré très tard chez moi et le lendemain j'étais très fatigué. J'ai envie d'y retourner parce que ça m'a vraiment inspiré.

Yesterday I was lucky because my friends and I went to London to see a concert. It was a school trip with all my friends who study music. The music was extraordinary, and I loved it. I got home very late and the next day I was very tired. I would like to go back there because it really inspired me.

Clubs after school

A mon collège on peut faire de la natation, jouer au foot ou au badminton et il y a des clubs d'échecs, de foot et de lecture. J'ai de la chance parce que je ne m'ennuie jamais. Moi je fais de l'aviron le samedi et je joue au tennis pour mon équipe scolaire.

At my school you can do swimming, play football or badminton and there are chess, football and reading clubs. I'm lucky because I never get bored. I do rowing on a Saturday and I play tennis for my school team.

Ideal school

Mon collège idéal serait grand, moderne, tout près de chez moi pour que je puisse y aller à pied. Il y aurait une énorme piscine et un cinéma. Les cours commenceraient à midi et termineraient à quinze heures. Il n'y aurait pas d'uniforme et on ne serait pas obligé d'aller au cours de maths.

My ideal school would be big, modern and very near my home so I could go there on foot. There would be an enormous swimming pool and a cinema. Lessons would begin at midday and would finish at 3pm. There would be no uniform and we wouldn't have to go to maths lessons.

What you'd change if you could

Si je pouvais changer quelque chose, je changerais l'uniforme car il est ennuyeux de porter la même chose tous les jours. Je voudrais plutôt porter un jean et un pull. En plus, je changerais l'horaire scolaire et l'emploi du temps, parce que les scientifiques ont prouvé que les ados ont besoin de plus de sommeil le matin. Si je pouvais commencer et terminer plus tard, je pourrais me concentrer mieux et j'aurais de meilleures notes.

If I could change something, I would change the uniform as it's boring wearing the same thing every day. I'd rather wear jeans and a jumper. Also, I would change the school timetable because scientists have proved that teenagers need more sleep in the mornings. If I could start and finish later, I would be able to concentrate better and I would get better grades.

Primary school

Quand j'étais plus jeune j'allais à une école primaire qui était petite, mais plus amicale et plus sympa que mon nouveau collège. Il n'y avait pas beaucoup de devoirs et on n'était pas obligé de porter un uniforme.

When I was younger I went to a primary school which was small but more friendly and nicer than my new school. There wasn't much homework and we didn't have to wear a uniform.

How will you celebrate the end of exams ?

Pour fêter la fin des examens j'irai chez Nandos avec tous mes amis, et après avoir mangé nous irons au cinéma pour regarder un film d'action. Ce sera super. Après le film je vais rentrer chez moi et dormir pendant quinze heures.

To celebrate the end of the exams I will go to Nandos with all my friends and after eating we will go to the cinema to see and action film. It will be great. After the film I will go home and sleep for 15 hours.

FUTURE EDUCATION AND WORK

Next year at school

Pour le bac, j'étudierai la géographie, la philosophie et l'économie parce que ce sont mes matières préférées et j'ai de bonnes notes. En plus, les profs sont sympas donc j'espère qu'ils ne nous donneront pas trop de devoirs. Je devrai travailler dur pendant les deux ans, bien que ce soit ennuyeux, pour que je puisse continuer mes études à l'université. Je voudrais aller à l'université d'Oxford pour étudier l'économie. Après avoir fini mes études, il faudra que je trouve un emploi où je peux gagner un énorme salaire, afin de pouvoir prendre la retraite à trente-cinq ans.

For my A levels I will study geography, philosophy and economics because they are my favourite subjects and I get good grades. Also, the teachers are nice so I I hope they won't give me too much homework. I will have to work hard over the two years although it's boring, so that I can continue my studies at university. I'd like to go to Oxford University to study economics. When I've finished studying I'll have to find a job where I can earn an enormous salary in order to be able to retire at 35.

Work experience

Je n'ai pas encore fait de stage en entreprise car je n'ai que seize ans, mais j'ai envie d'avoir l'occasion de travailler dans un cabinet juridique pour savoir si j'aimerais ce genre de boulot à l'avenir. C'est important que les jeunes aient de l'expérience du monde de travail pour qu'ils puissent se rendre compte de ce que font les adultes tous les jours.

I have not yet done any work experience as I am only 16, but I would like to have the chance to work in a law firm to see if I would like that kind of job in the future. It's important that young people have experience of the world of work so that they realise what adults do every day.

Weekend jobs

L'année dernière j'ai travaillé dans un restaurant pendant les grandes vacances. Je devais préparer les légumes, mettre les tables et servir les repas aux clients. Je nettoyais la cuisine chaque soir aussi. Ce n'était pas bien payé mais je recevais des pourboires tous les jours, donc j'ai pu économiser un peu d'argent. A mon avis il est utile d'avoir un petit job le week-end car on peut apprendre la valeur de l'argent, apprendre à travailler en équipe, à être responsable et communiquer efficacement avec les autres.

Last year I worked in a restaurant in the summer holidays. I had to prepare vegetables, lay the tables and serve meals to customers. I cleaned the kitchen every evening too. It wasn't well-paid but I received tips every day, so I was able to save a bit of money. In my opinion it's useful to have a little weekend job as you can learn the value of money, learn to work in a team, to be responsible and communicate effectively with others.

Future job

Je ne sais pas encore ce que je vais faire mais il faut que ce soit intéressant et passionnant. Avant tout je voudrais gagner tous les tournois de tennis et être champion du monde. Sinon, j'aimerais être prof pour que je puisse profiter des longues vacances. De plus, je voudrais travailler avec les jeunes car c'est plus enrichissant que bosser dans un bureau.

I don't know yet what I'm going to do but it's got to be interesting and exciting. Above all I would like to win all the tennis tournaments and be world champion. Otherwise I'd like to be a teacher so I can make the most of the long holiday. What's more, I'd like to work with young people because it's more gratifying than working in an office.

Ideal job

Je voudrais bien travailler à l'étranger pour améliorer mon français et mon espagnol. Après avoir étudié pendant autant d'années ce serait dommage de tout abandonner. En plus, si je suis champion de tennis je vais devoir voyager! Mon emploi idéal serait joueur de tennis professionnel – c'est mon rêve tout simplement. A mon avis c'est important de suivre ses rêves, même si on ne réussit pas. Il faut au moins qu'on essaie.

I would like to work abroad to improve my French and Spanish. After studying for so many years it would be a shame to give it all up. Also, if I'm world tennis champion I will have to travel! My ideal job would be professional tennis player – that's just my dream. I think it's important to follow your dreams, even if you don't succeed. You have to try at least.

How to get a job

Pour trouver un emploi, il faut d'abord poser sa candidature, en remplissant des fiches, avant d'assister à un entretien / interview, qui est souvent en ligne au premier tour. Si on réussit, on assiste à un interview en personne. C'est un procès épuisant !

To find a job, you have to apply by filling in forms before attending an interview which is often online for the first round. If you succeed, you go to an interview in person. It's an exhausting process!

Unemployment

Malheureusement, il y a un grand problème de chômage en Angleterre, surtout chez les jeunes qui viennent de terminer leurs études, et si on n'est diplomé, on peut avoir du mal à trouver un boulot. J'ai horreur d'être au chômage à l'avenir. Les chômeurs risquent d'être atteints de la dépression et ne reçoivent que de ridicules allocations qui ne s'étendent même pas aux factures, et je ne parle même pas de vacances.

Unfortunately, there is a big unemployment problem in England, especially for young people who have just finished school, and if you're not sufficiently qualified you can struggle to find a job. I am terrified of being unemployed in the future. The unemployed are at risk of depression and only get very small benefits which don't even cover the bills, not to mention holidays.

HOUSE, HOME AND DAILY ROUTINES

Describe your house

J'habite une grande maison avec un jardin à l'arrière. Elle est ancienne et jolie, avec cinq chambres et deux salles de bain. J'aime ma maison parce que c'est confortable et il y a tout ce dont j'ai besoin, je ne suis pas obligé de partager ma chambre et ce n'est pas loin de mon école.

I live in a big house with a garden at the back. It's old and beautiful, with 5 bedrooms and two bathrooms. I like my house because it's comfortable and there is everything I need, I don't have to share a bedroom and it's not far from my school.

Describe your bedroom

Ma chambre est assez grande avec des murs bleus. Devant la porte se trouve mon lit et à côté il y a mon armoire et une étagère. J'aime ma chambre parce qu'il y a tout ce dont j'ai besoin, c'est confortable et bleu est ma couleur préférée. De plus, je ne dois plus la partager avec mon frère – quelle chance !

My bedroom is quite big with blue walls. In front of the door is my bed and next to it there is my wardrobe and a bookshelf. I like my room because there is everything I need, it's comfortable and blue is my favourite colour. What's more, I no longer have to share it with my brother – how lucky!

Ideal house

Ma maison idéale serait énorme avec deux grandes piscines et beaucoup de chambres pour que mes amis puissent m'y rendre visite. Aussi, il y aurait un spa et un gymnase pour que je puisse rester en forme et un court de tennis ou je pourrais m'entrainer. Il y aurait un grand jardin avec beaucoup de fleurs et des arbres. Il faut que ce soit situé dans une ville animée comme Londres.

My ideal house would be enormous with two big swimming pools and lots of bedrooms so my friends could come and visit me. Also there would be a spa and a gym so I could keep fit and a tennis court where I could train. There would be a big garden with lots of flowers and trees. I would have to be situated in a lively town like London.

Daily routine - week

Normalement pendant la semaine je me lève à sept heures, je me douche, je prends mon petit déjeuner et je quitte la maison à huit heures. J'arrive au collège à huit heures et demie, et je rentre à quatre heures. Chez moi, le soir, je fais mes devoirs, je prends mon diner en regardant la télé et je me couche vers dix heures.

Normally during the week I get up at 7, I shower, have breakfast and leave the house at 8. I arrive at school at 8.30 and I come home at 4. At home in the evening I do my homework, have my dinner watching TV and go to bed around 10.

Daily routine – weekend

Normalement le week-end je me lève plus tard que normalement, je me douche et je me brosse les dents. Je prends mon petit déjeuner et je quitte la maison à neuf heures pour aller à mon club de tennis. Je rentre chez moi à midi, et après avoir mangé je fais mes devoirs. Normalement je sors avec mes amis, au cinéma ou au parc, et puis je prends mon diner en regardant la télé. Puis je télécharge de la musique, ou bien je mets à jour mon profil Facebook et je bavarde sur le web avec mes copains. Je me couche vers dix heures mais souvent j'ai du mal à m'endormir donc je lis mon livre avant d'éteindre la lumière.

Normally at the weekend I get up later than usual, I shower and brush my teeth. I have breakfast and I leave the house at 9 to go to my tennis club. I come home at 12 and after eating I do my homework. Normally I go out with my friends to the cinema or the park and then I have my dinner watching TV. Then I download music or update my Facebook profile and I chat online with my friends. I go to bed around 10 but often I find it hard to go to sleep so I read my book before turning the light off.

This morning
Ce matin je me suis levé à six heures parce que je devais préparer mon examen oral de français. Je me suis douché et j'ai pris mon petit déjeuner avant de quitter la maison. Je suis arrivé au collège à huit heures et demie et j'ai bavardé avec mes copains.

This morning I got up at 6 because I had to revise for my French oral exam. I showered and had breakfast before leaving the house. I arrived at school at 8.30 and I chatted with my friends.

This evening
Ce soir je vais me détendre, car demain je n'aurai pas d'examens. Je vais regarder la télé et prendre mon diner avec mes parents. Ils vont m'interroger sur mon examen et je ne leur en dirai rien du tout !

Tonight I'm going to relax as I won't have any exams tomorrow. I am going to watch TV and have dinner with my parents. They will ask me all about my exam and I won't tell them anything at all.

What you would change about your routine
Si je pouvais changer quelque chose, je voudrais me lever plus tard et commencer l'école à midi, car je suis toujours fatigué le matin, et

les scientifiques ont prouvé que les ados ont besoin de plus de sommeil le matin.

If I could change something, I would like to get up later and start school at midday as I'm always tired in the mornings, and the scientists have proved that teenagers need more sleep in the morning.

Helping at home
Pour aider à la maison je range ma chambre de temps en temps, je fais la vaisselle et je mets la table, mais je ne fais pas beaucoup parce que normalement j'ai trop de devoirs. Je pense que c'est important d'aider avec le ménage mais les devoirs sont plus importants, surtout juste avant les examens.

To help at home I tidy my room sometimes, I do the washing up and I lay the table, but I don't do much because normally I have too much homework. I think it's important to help with housework, but homework is more important, especially just before the exams.

Help at home yesterday
Hier j'ai mis la table pour donner un coup de main à ma mère, mais rien de plus car j'ai dû préparer mon examen de français.

Yesterday I laid the table and nothing else as I had to prepare for my French exam.

Cooking at home
Normalement c'est ma mère qui fait la cuisine. Elle prépare le diner pendant que je suis au collège, mais parfois si elle n'est pas là je prépare quelque chose comme les pâtes. Aussi j'adore faire des gâteaux parce que j'aime les manger !

Normally my mother does the cooking. She makes the dinner while I'm at school, but sometimes if she's not there I make something like pasta. Also, I love making cakes because I like eating them.

Plans for next weekend with family

Le week-end prochain j'ai envie d'aller au cinéma pour voir le nouveau film d'action. Ma mère a envie de le voir aussi. Après ça nous irons chez Starbucks pour prendre un chocolat chaud et discuter du film. Puis je rentrerai chez moi pour que je puisse manger avant d'aller à mon club de tennis pour m'entrainer pour mon prochain concours. Le soir je vais manger des pâtes et de la glace parce que j'aurai une faim de loup.

Next weekend I want to go to the cinema to see the new action film. My mother wants to see it as well. After that we will go to Starbucks for a hot chocolate and to discuss the film. Then I will go back home so I can eat before going to my tennis club to train for my next competition. In the evening I am going to eat pasta and ice cream because I will be ravenous.

Last weekend with your family

Le week-end dernier nous sommes allés au parc pour promener le chien / jouer au foot, puis nous avions faim, donc nous sommes allés au restaurant près de chez moi et nous avons pris le déjeuner en bavardant. Après avoir mangé nous sommes rentrés et nous avons regardé un film ensemble. Ça fait du bien de passer du temps avec ma famille car on s'entend très bien et on s'amuse ensemble.

Last weekend we went to the park to walk the dog / play football, then we were hungry, so we went to a restaurant near my house and had lunch while chatting. After eating we went home and watched a film together. It feels good to spend time with my family as we get on very well and we have fun together.

FOOD, HEALTH AND HOBBIES

What you eat for breakfast
Au petit déjeuner je ne prends que des céréales et du jus d'orange car je n'ai jamais faim le matin.

For breakfast I only have cereal and orange juice as I am never hungry in the morning.

General eating habits
En général je mange sainement pour rester en forme parce que je suis sportif, mais mon repas préféré c'est la pizza car c'est délicieux et facile à préparer, suivi par de la glace au chocolat. Bien que ce soit malsain, c'est le meilleur repas du monde.

In general I eat healthily to stay fit because I'm sporty, but my favourite meal is pizza because it's delicious and easy to make, followed by chocolate icecream. Although it's unhealthy it's the best meal in the world.

What don't you like eating ?
Il n'y a rien que je n'aime pas manger mais je n'aime pas tellement les champignons.

There is nothing I don't like eating but I don't like mushrooms much.

Lunch at school
Je prends mon diner à la cantine au collège et pour la plupart c'est assez bon, mais de temps en temps les légumes sont trop cuits. Hier j'ai mangé du poulet avec des frites et des petits pois. C'était délicieux.

I have lunch in the school canteen and for the most part it's quite good but sometimes the vegetables are overcooked. Yesterday I ate chicken with chips and peas. It was delicious.

Favourite food

J'adore la cuisine Italienne parce que je la trouve délicieuse et nous allons assez souvent à mon restaurant préféré parce que la pizza est à tomber. La dernière fois que j'y suis allé, j'ai autant mangé que je n'ai presque pas pu me lever de la table. J'ai eu les yeux plus gros que le ventre.

I love Italian food because I find it delicious and we quite often go to my favourite restaurant because the pizza is to die for. Last time I went there I at so much I could hardly get up from the table. My eyes were bigger than my stomach

How to be healthy

Pour rester en forme il faut manger plein de légumes et de fruits, il faut boire huit verres d'eau par jour et éviter le sucre et la matière grasse, et bien sur l'alcool et le tabac. Il faut aussi faire de l'exercice et passer du temps en plein air.

To stay healthy, you have to eat lots of vegetables and fruit, you have to drink 8 glasses of water a day and avoid sugar and fat, and of course alcohol and tobacco. You should also do exercise and spend time in the fresh air.

Why good health is important to you

Pour moi c'est important de rester en forme car je joue au tennis plusieurs fois par semaine. J'y joue depuis cinq ans, j'y suis accro et je ne pourrais pas m'en passer. C'est le meilleur sport du monde. Donc pour la plupart je mange sainement et j'essaie d'éviter le sucre et la matière grasse, mais ce n'est pas toujours facile car j'adore le chocolat. En plus je bois un litre d'eau par jour. Je n'ai jamais fumé et je n'aime pas l'alcool. Peut-être que ça changera à l'avenir mais j'ai de bonnes intentions !

It's important to me to keep fit as I play tennis several times a week. I've been playing for 5 years, I am addicted to it and I couldn't manage without it. It's the best sport in the world. So for the most part I eat healthily and I try to avoid sugar and fat but it's not always easy as I love chocolate. I also drink a litre of water a day, I have never smoked and I don't like alcohol. Maybe that will change in the future but I have good intentions!

Staying healthy in the future

Quand je serai adulte je vais continuer à faire du sport, bien que ce soit fatigant, afin de pouvoir rester en forme et éviter les maladies comme l'obésité et le diabète. Je vais m'abonner à un centre sportif et passer tout mon temps libre à m'entrainer.

When I'm older I'm going to carry on doing sport, although it's tiring, so that I can keep fit and avoid illnesses like obesity and diabetes. I will join a fitness club and spend all my free time training.

Sickness

J'ai de la chance parce que je ne tombe malade que très rarement. Normalement si ce n'est pas grave, il faut rester au lit mais si tu ne vas pas mieux après quelques jours il faut aller chez le médecin, qui te donnera des médicaments ou des comprimés.

I'm lucky because I only very rarely get ill. Normally if it's not serious you have to stay in bed but if you're not better after a few days you have to go to the doctor who will give you medicine or pills.

Smoking

Pour moi, fumer c'est ridicule, car on sait que ça raccourcit la vie et ça entraine de graves maladies comme le cancer.   Je ne fumerai jamais. Je pense que les ados commencent à fumer pour de diverses raisons. La raison principale c'est la pression du groupe. Si on va à une soirée il y a toujours des ados qui fument sans que leurs parents ne le sachent et il y aura toujours des autres qui veulent faire partie du groupe, mais pas moi non.

For me, smoking is ridiculous as we know it shortens your life and causes serious illnesses like cancer. I will never smoke. I think young people start smoking for a variety of reasons. The main reason is peer pressure. If you go to a party there are always teenagers smoking without their parents' knowledge and there will always be others who want to be part of the group, but not me.

Alcohol

Pour moi, l'alcool c'est ridicule, car on sait que ça raccourcit la vie et ça entraine de graves maladies comme le cancer et les crises cardiaques. Je ne boirai jamais. Je pense que les ados commencent à boire pour de diverses raisons. La raison principale c'est la pression du groupe. Si on va à une soirée il y a toujours des ados qui boivent sans que leurs parents ne le sachent et il y aura toujours des autres qui veulent faire partie du groupe, mais pas moi non.

For me, alcohol is ridiculous as we know it shortens your life and causes serious illnesses like cancer and heart attacks. I will never drink. I think young people start drinking for a variety of reasons. The main reason is peer pressure. If you go to a party there are always teenagers drinking without their parents' knowledge and there will always be others who want to be part of the group, but not me.

Drugs

Pour moi, les drogues sont ridicules, car on sait que ça raccourcit la vie et ça entraine de graves maladies comme le cancer. Je n'en prendrai jamais. Je pense que les ados commencent à se droguer pour de diverses raisons. La raison principale c'est la pression du groupe. Si on va à une soirée il y a toujours des ados qui se droguent sans que leurs parents ne le sachent et il y aura toujours des autres qui veulent faire partie du groupe, mais pas moi non.

For me, drugs are ridiculous as we know it shortens your life and causes serious illnesses like cancer. I will never take any. I think young people start taking drugs for a variety of reasons. The main reason is peer pressure. If you go to a party there are always teenagers taking drugs without their parents' knowledge and there will always be others who want to be part of the group, but not me.

Vegetarianism

Je pense que les gens deviennent végétariens pour de diverses raisons. Normalement c'est parce qu'ils ne veulent pas tuer les animaux, mais il y a des gens qui le font pour des raisons de santé, ou bien pour des raisons environnementales. On dit que si on arrêtait de détruire les forêts tropicales en sud-Amérique pour y mettre des vaches, la planète aurait plus de chance de survivre. Le bœuf n'est pas aussi important qu'il faille sacrifier notre monde.

I think that people become vegetarian for a variety of reasons. Normally it's because they don't want to kill animals, but there are people who do it for reasons of health or for environmental reasons. They say that if we stopped destroying the tropical forests in South America to graze cows, the planet would have a better chance of surviving. Beef is not so important that we have to sacrifice our world.

Sport and hobbies

Je suis accro au sport parce que c'est amusant, énergique et bon pour la santé physique et mentale. Je joue au tennis deux fois par semaine. J'ai de la chance parce que je suis membre d'un club de tennis depuis cinq ans et je fais partie de l'équipe scolaire. En plus je joue au foot et au rugby et je fais de l'athlétisme. Pendant les vacances je fais du vélo avec mon père.

I'm addicted to sport because it's fun, energetic and good for your physical and mental health. I play tennis twice a week. I'm lucky because I have been a member of a tennis club for five years and I am in my school team. I also play football and rugby and I do athletics. During the holidays I go cycling with my father.

Hobbies when you were young
Quand j'étais jeune je faisais moins de sport mais je passais la plupart de mon temps à jouer dans le parc avec mes amis. En plus, je regardais la télévision et je jouais aux jeux de société avec ma famille.

When I was young I did less sport but I spent most of my time playing in the park with my friends. I also used to watch TV and play board games with my family.

Music and musicians
Je ne joue pas d'instrument mais j'aime la musique. Le style que je préfère c'est le rock, car c'est très fort et il y a beaucoup d'instruments, c'est énergique et ça me fait plaisir de l'écouter. J'ai envie de voir mon chanteur préféré, Ed Sheeran en concert mais il faut que je fasse des tâches ménagères chez moi pour gagner l'argent pour payer l'entrée. C'est comme ça que ça marche chez moi. J'aime Ed Sheeran parce qu'il est tellement doué et sa voix me donne un frisson quand je l'écoute. Il m'a inspiré parce qu'il vient d'une famille pauvre et il a travaillé toute sa vie pour réussir.

I don't play an instrument but I like music. The type I prefer is rock as it's very loud and there are lots of instruments, it's energetic and it makes me happy listening to it. I'd like to see my favourite singer Ed Sheeran in concert but I have to do housework to earn the money to buy the tickets. That's how it works at my house. I like Ed Sheeran because he's so talented and his voice gives me goose bumps when I listen to him. He has inspired me because he comes from a poor family and he worked all his life to succeed.

Ideal weekend

Mon week-end idéal serait chez moi avec ma famille et mes amis. Je jouerais au foot dans le jardin, j'irais au cinéma pour voir un film d'action et je mangerais dans un bon restaurant. Le lendemain j'irais à la piscine pour faire de la natation et après être rentré chez moi je regarderais un film sur Netflix, en mangeant des bonbons.

My ideal weekend would be at home with my family and friends. I would play football in the garden, I'd go to the cinema to see an action film and I'd eat in a good restaurant. The next day I'd go to the pool to swim and after coming home I would watch a film on Netflix while eating sweets.

Books you've read

Je lis des livres de temps en temps mais pas assez souvent. Je suis en train de lire 'Child 44'. Il s'agit d'un garçon en Russie qui grandit en pauvreté mais qui commence à travailler pour le KGB. C'est super-passionnant. Le suspense m'a tenu en haleine jusqu'à la fin.

I read books from time to time but not often enough. I'm in the middle of reading Child 44. It's about a boy in Russia who grows up in poverty but who starts working for the KGB. It's very exciting. I was on the edge of my seat right to the end.

Do you watch TV?

Je ne regarde jamais la télé parce que les profs nous donnent trop de devoirs donc je n'ai pas le temps, mais j'écoute la radio parfois en faisant mes devoirs. Si jamais j'ai du temps libre, je préfère regarder un film sur Netflix.

*I never watch TV because the teachers give us too much homework
so I don't have the time, but I listen to the radio sometimes while
doing my homework. If every I have free time I prefer to watch a film
on Netflix.*

Young people and TV

C'est vrai que les jeunes regardent beaucoup de télé, mais je pense
que le problème est plutôt qu'ils passent trop de temps devant les
écrans à jouer aux jeux-vidéo. Ce serait mieux de regarder la télé,
parce que là au moins il y a des émissions éducatives, les infos, des
documentaires etcetera.

*It's true that young people watch a lot of TV but I think that the
problem is more that they spend too much time in front of screens
playing video games. It would be better to watch TV because there
at least there are educational programmes, news, documentaries etc.*

Your favourite type of TV programme

À mon avis, les feuilletons sont les meilleures émissions parce
qu'elles sont captivantes et grisantes. Elles me font rire et pleurer. Si
j'avais plus de temps libre j'en regarderais plus mais les profs nous
donnent trop de devoirs.

*In my opinion, soaps are the best programmes because they are
exciting and intoxicating, they make me laugh and cry. If I had more
free time I'd watch more of them but the teachers give us too much
homework.*

Your favourite type of film

Je dirais que je préfère les films d'action parce qu'il y a de bons
effets spéciaux. Ils sont plus passionnants que les films romantiques
et moins effrayants que les films d'horreur.

*I would say that I prefer action films because there are good special
effects. They are more exciting than romance films and less scary
than horror films.*

The last film you saw

Le dernier film que j'ai vu était la Mort de Stalin. C'était une comédie, mais je ne l'ai pas trouvé drôle, donc j'ai été un peu déçue. Cependant, j'ai appris quelque chose sur l'histoire de la Russie donc ça a valu la peine d'y aller. Les acteurs ont super-bien joué. J'ai préféré Maze Runner que j'ai vu l'année dernière. J'étais scotché à l'écran jusqu'au dernier moment du film.

The last film I saw was the Death of Stalin. It was a comedy but I didn't find it funny so I was a bit disappointed. However, I learnt something about the history of Russia so it was worth going. The actors played really well. I preferred Maze Runner which I saw last year. I was glued to the screen until the last moment of the film.

French films you have seen

J'ai vu un film français qui s'appelle 'Les Choristes', un film de Christophe Barratier. C'est l'histoire d'un prof de musique dans un internat de rééducation. En enseignant le chant choral, il réussit à transformer la vie des garçons. Je l'ai trouvé amusant et triste en même temps.

I saw a French film called "the choristers", a Christophe Barratier film. It's the story of a music teacher in a boarding school. By teaching choral singing he manages to transform the lives of the boys. I found it fun and sad at the same time

Cinema or TV ?

Je préfère le cinéma parce que c'est plus passionnant que rester dans le salon. J'aime les films d'action parce qu'il y a de bons effets spéciaux. Cependant, les billets coutent les yeux de la tête et je n'ai pas les moyens d'y aller plus qu'une fois par mois.

I prefer the cinema because it's more exciting that staying in the living room. I like action films because there are good special effects. However, the tickets cost the earth and I can't afford to go more than once a month.

Pocket money and shopping

Moi je déteste faire du shopping et je ne le fais jamais, sauf quand je suis obligé d'acheter de nouveaux vêtements parce que là, ma mère ne sait pas mon goût. Je reçois dix livres par semaine mais j'essaie d'économiser mon argent au lieu de le gaspiller. La dernière chose que j'ai achetée c'est les billets de cinéma pour Star Wars. Ça valait la peine. C'était excellent ! Quant aux courses, ma mère fait tout en ligne.

I hate shopping and I never do it, except when I have to buy new clothes because my mother doesn't know my taste. I receive ten pounds a week but I try to save my money instead of wasting it. The last thing I bought was cinema tickets for Star Wars. It was worth it. It was excellent! As for food shopping, my mother does it all on line.

IDENTITY AND RELATIONSHIPS

About you

J'ai quinze / seize ans. Je suis de taille moyenne, j'ai les cheveux blonds et les yeux bleus. Je suis très marrant, sportif et assez intelligent mais parfois un peu paresseux, surtout le matin quand je n'ai pas envie d'aller au collège.

I'm 15/16 years old. I am medium height, I have blond hair and blue eyes. I am very funny, sporty, and quite intelligent but sometimes a bit lazy, especially in the mornings when I don't want to go to school.

Describe your family

Il y a quatre personnes dans ma famille – mon père, ma mère, ma sœur et moi. Normalement on s'entend bien mais de temps en temps on se dispute. Ma sœur s'appelle Emily et elle a quatorze ans. Elle a les cheveux longs et blonds et les yeux marron. Elle est moins sportive que moi, elle est têtue et casse-pieds mais au moins on n'est pas obligé de partager une chambre. Ma mère est gentille et plus timide que mon père, qui n'arrête pas de faire l'andouille. J'en ai ras le bol !

There are 4 people in my family, my father, my mother, my two sisters and me. Normally we get on well but from time to time we argue. My sister is called Emily and she is 14. She has long blond hair and brown eyes. She is less sporty than me, she's stubborn and annoying but at least we don't have to share a room. My mother is kind and more introverted than my father who is always messing about. I've had enough of it!

The ideal family

Je ne pense pas qu'il y ait une famille idéale. Il y a toutes sortes de familles dans le monde, y compris les familles recomposées et monoparentales. L'important c'est que la famille passe du temps ensemble et que les enfants grandissent avec de la confiance et l'amour. J'ai de la chance parce que je trouve que ma famille est presqu'idéale.

I don't think there is such a thing as an ideal family. There are all sorts of families in the world including merged families and one parent families. The important thing is that the family spends time together and that the children grow up with confidence and love. I'm lucky because I think my family is almost ideal.

The importance of marriage

A mon avis, le mariage n'est pas important, car on peut vivre avec un partenaire sans se marier, mais ça dépend de son point de vue. Il y a certains qui ont besoin de sécurité et des autres qui ont peur que ça tombe mal après quelques années – et tout le monde sait que le divorce coute les yeux de la tête. L'important c'est que tout le monde puisse se marier, peu importe leur orientation sexuelle. Heureusement, la loi a enfin changé et on peut aussi choisir le pacte civil au lieu du mariage si on veut éviter les frais du divorce. Moi, je ne sais pas si je vais me marier ou non. Je suis trop jeune pour prendre une telle décision.

In my opinion marriage is not important as one can live with a partner without getting married, but it depends on your viewpoint. There are some people who need security and others who are afraid that things will go wrong after a few years – and everyone knows that divorce costs a fortune. The important thing is that everyone can get married regardless of their sexual orientation. Luckily, the law has finally changed and you can also choose the civil partnership instead of marriage if you want to avoid the costs of divorce. I don't know if I want to get married or not. I'm too young to take such a decision.

Describe your best friend
Mon meilleur ami s'appelle James et il a les cheveux bruns et les yeux marron. Il est sportif et marrant et il me fait rire tout le temps. Ce que j'aime c'est que nous avons beaucoup de choses en commun, et il est toujours là pour moi.   Cependant, quand j'ai envie d'être seul ça ne le dérange pas. Nous avons tous les deux beaucoup de copains et on ne dépend pas l'un de l'autre.

My best friend is called James and he has brown hair and brown eyes. He is sporty and funny and he makes me laugh all the time. What I like is that we have lots of things in common and he is always there for me. However, when I feel like being on my own that doesn't bother him. We both have lots of friends and we don't depend on each other.

Best friend – future outings
Ce weekend on ira au cinéma avec des autres amis pour voir le nouveau film de Star Wars. J'ai hâte de le voir car j'ai entendu qu'il y a de bons effets spéciaux. Cette année il viendra en Espagne avec nous. Ce sera parfait.

This weekend we are going to go to the cinema with some other friends to see the new Star Wars film. I'm looking forward to seeing it because I have heard that there are good special effects. This year he is coming to Spain with us. It will be perfect.

Role models

Un modèle à suivre devrait donner un bon exemple en tout. Il devrait être gentil, compréhensif, intelligent, et ne devrait pas être parfait. Il faut que les jeunes apprennent à se respecter sans se comparer aux autres, et il faut suivre des modèles qui montrent qu'il y a des choses plus importantes dans la vie.

A role model should give a good example in everything. They should be kind, understanding, intelligent and should not be perfect. Young people need to learn to respect themselves without comparing themselves to others, and one should have role models who show that there are more important things in life.

Importance of your birthday

J'adore mon anniversaire. C'est la date la plus importante de l'année car je reçois plein de cadeaux et mes parents font tout pour que je puisse me détendre et faire tout ce que je veux.

I love my birthday. It's the most important date of the year as I receive lots of presents and my parents do everything so I can relax and do everything I want.

Your last birthday

Pour fêter mon dernier anniversaire, je suis allé au restaurant avec ma famille et j'ai mangé mon repas préféré, la pizza. C'était super et je me suis bien amusé. Cependant après avoir mangé je suis rentré chez moi et, quelle désastre – le chien avait mangé mon gâteau d'anniversaire ! On a dû aller en chercher un autre au magasin.

To celebrate my last birthday I went to the restaurant with my family and I ate my favourite meal, pizza. It was great and I had a lot of fun. However, after eating, I went home and, what a disaster, the dog had eaten my birthday cake. We had to go and get another one from the shop.

ENVIRONMENT, SOCIETY AND GLOBAL ISSUES

Global problems

A mon avis les plus gros problèmes mondiaux sont la pauvreté et l'environnement. Il est tellement triste de voir les SDF qui sont obligés de dormir dans les rues des grandes villes des pays riches, et de voir comment la famine et la corruption ont détruit des pays africains. Également, je m'inquiète de l'avenir de la planète, car bientôt il ne restera plus de ressources naturelles.

In my view the biggest world problems are poverty and the environment. It is so sad to see the homeless who have to sleep in the streets of the big cities in rich countries, and to see how famine and corruption have destroyed African countries. Also, I worry about the future of the planet as soon we are going to run out of natural resources.

Volunteering

Tout le monde devrait faire du bénévolat pour aider les démunis. Le gouvernement n'a pas les moyens de faire tout ce qui est nécessaire. Moi, je voudrais trouver un boulot a mi-temps dans une association caritative pour les SDF. J'ai déjà aidé à collecter des fonds en organisant un match de foot a mon collège entre les profs et les élèves. C'est super de savoir que l'on fait une différence.

Everyone should do volunteering to help the less fortunate. The government can't afford to do everything that's necessary. I'd like to find a part-time job in a charity for the homeless. I have already helped to collect funds by organizing a football match between the teachers and the pupils at my school. It's great to know that you're making a difference.

Climate change

Le climat est en train de changer, il n'y a aucun doute. Il ne neige plus en hiver, tandis que pendant les années quatre-vingt il neigeait souvent. Le réchauffement de la terre a déjà causé l'augmentation du niveau des océans et il y a des iles qui commencent à disparaitre. En plus il y a de plus en plus d'ouragans et de tempêtes. Je trouve tout ça effrayant, car il me semble que c'est en cherchant une meilleure vie que nous détruisons notre planète.

There is no doubt that climate change is happening. It doesn't snow anymore in winter, whereas in the 80s it snowed a lot. Global warming has already caused ocean levels to rise and some islands are disappearing. Also, there are more and more hurricanes and storms. I find all that frightening, as it seems to me that it is in searching for a better life that we are destroying our planet.

Climate change solution

Il faut qu'on fasse des efforts pour changer nos habitudes, consommer moins, voyager moins, gaspiller moins d'énergie et utiliser l'énergie renouvelable comme l'énergie solaire et éolienne. On devrait utiliser les transports en commun, recycler plus et construire plus de pistes cyclables pour encourager les gens à abandonner leurs voitures.

We've got to make an effort to change our habits, consume less, travel less, waste less energy and use renewable energy like solar and wind power. We should be using public transport, doing more recycling and building more cycle paths to encourage people to leave their cars at home.

What you do for the environment personally

Je fais beaucoup pour protéger l'environnement. Je prends une douche au lieu d'un bain pour économiser l'eau, j'éteins la lumière quand je quitte une pièce pour économiser l'électricité, je recycle les emballages comme le carton, le papier, le verre et le plastique, j'utilise le transport en commun et j'achète des produits écologiques.

I do a lot to protect the environment. I shower instead of having a bath to save water, I switch off the light when I leave a room to save electricity, I recycle packaging like cardboard, paper, glass and plastic, I use public transport and I buy green products.

What you do for the environment at school
Au collège, tout le monde fait beaucoup d'efforts pour protéger l'environnement. On a des poubelles de recyclage dans toutes les salles de classe, on éteint les lumières quand on sort d'une pièce, et on encourage les élèves à prendre le bus au lieu de la voiture pour aller au collège.

At school everyone makes a big effort to protect the environment. We have recycling bins in all the classrooms, we turn off the lights when we leave a room and the pupils are encouraged to use public transport instead of the car to travel to school.

What's the biggest environmental problem and what causes it?
Je pense que la pollution atmosphérique, c'est le problème le plus grave auquel on fait face en ce moment. Le problème c'est que les émissions des voitures et des usines causent la pollution de l'air, l'effet de serre, le réchauffement de la terre. J'en ai marre, et j'ai peur que quand je serai adulte ce sera difficile de respirer dans les grandes villes.

I think air pollution is the most serious problem we are facing at the moment. The problem is that the car and factory emissions cause the air pollution, the greenhouse effect and global warming. I'm sick of it and I'm afraid that when I'm older it will be difficult to breathe in the big cities.

Consequences of not protecting the environment

Si on ne protège pas la planète, il n'y aura bientôt plus de ressources naturelles, le trou dans la couche d'ozone grandira, et la race humaine disparaitra. Il faut qu'on fasse des efforts pour éviter cet avenir avant que ce ne soit trop tard.

If we don't protect the planet, soon we will run out of natural resources, the hole in the ozone layer will get bigger and the human race will disappear. We need to make an effort to avoid this outcome before it's too late.

The importance of the news

Les infos sont importantes parce qu'il faut qu'on sache ce qui se passe dans le monde pour avoir une opinion là-dessus. Si on n'est pas suffisamment informé, on peut être berné par les médias.

News is important because we need to know what's going on in the world in order to have an opinion on it. If you're not well-informed enough you can get brainwashed by the media.

What's in the news at the moment?

Actuellement c'est le climat qui fait la une - il y a des inondations partout, des tremblements de terre et des ouragans et des centaines de maisons ont été détruites. En plus il y a la menace constante de pandémie, après la mort des centaines de gens du Coronavirus.

Right now it's climate that's making the headlines – there are floods everywhere, earthquakes and hurricanes and hundreds of houses have been destroyed. Also there is the constant threat of pandemic after the deaths of hundreds of people from Coronavirus.

Do you read a paper ?

Je ne lis pas de journal, parce que je trouve que c'est plus vite en ligne et j'ai l'application de la BBC sur mon portable.

L'application me prévient chaque fois qu'il y a quelque chose d'important à savoir.

I don't read a paper because I find it's faster online and I have the BBC app on my phone. The app notifies me every time there's something important to know.

Which is the most popular newspaper?
Je pense que les journaux les plus populaires ce sont les journaux de petit format, les journaux à sensation. Ils ne contiennent rien d'intéressant, et ils ne servent qu'à faire peur aux, en disant que le gouvernement est nul, que tout est un désastre. Je déteste ces journaux.

I think that the most popular newspapers are the sensationalist tabloids. They don't have anything interesting in them and all they do is frighten people, saying that the government is no good, that everything is a disaster. I hate those newspapers.

Importance of advertising
Je trouve la publicité nécessaire pour l'économie, car les entreprises en ont besoin pour se faire connaitre. Cependant, la pub pour la malbouffe devrait être interdite comme la pub pour les cigarettes, car elles sont tellement mauvaises pour la santé.

I think that advertising is necessary for the economy as companies need it to make themselves known. However, advertising junk food should be banned like advertising cigarettes as they are so bad for the health.

TECHNOLOGY

Mobile phones – do you have one and why ?

Oui, j'ai un portable dont je me sers tous les jours – pour rester en contact avec mes parents, mes amis, pour envoyer des textos et pour mettre à jour mon statut sur Facebook. Je ne pourrais pas m'en passer, j'y suis tout à fait accro.

Yes I have a mobile that I use every day – to stay in touch with my parents, my friends, to send texts and to update my Facebook status. I couldn't do without it, I'm completely addicted to it.

Young people and mobile phones

Les jeunes aiment les portables parce qu'ils sont tellement utiles, pour rester en contact avec ses amis sur les réseaux sociaux, pour envoyer les textos et pour surfer le web, écouter de la musique, prendre des photos et jouer aux jeux sur les applications.

Young people like mobile phones because they are so useful, to stay in touch with friends, to send texts and use the internet, to listen to music, take photos and play games on apps.

Dangers of mobile phones

Le danger principal c'est qu'on peut perdre beaucoup de temps en faisant tout ça, et devenir accro au portable. Aussi, si on traverse la rue en regardant son portable on pourrait facilement avoir un accident. De plus il y a le risque de vol d'identité et de cyber intimidation sur les réseaux sociaux.

The main danger is that you can waste a lot of time doing all that, and become addicted to the phone. Also if you cross the road looking at your phone you could easily have an accident. There is also the risk of identity theft and online bullying on social networks.

Importance of computers / internet

L'ordinateur c'est indispensable pour moi et je pense qu'à l'avenir ils seront de plus en plus importants pour tout le monde. On ne pourra pas travailler sans ordinateur. Je l'ai utilisé hier soir pour faire mes devoirs et pour envoyer des mails. Le plus grand avantage de l'ordinateur c'est que c'est le meilleur moyen de surfer le web et d'accéder à l'internet. Avec internet on peut communiquer avec les gens à l'étranger face à face sur Skype, on peut télécharger des films et de la musique, on peut envoyer des messages sur les réseaux sociaux et faire du commerce.

The computer is essential to me and I think that in the future they will be more and more important for everyone. We won't be able to work without a computer. I used it last night to do my homework and to send emails. The biggest advantage of the computer is that it's the best way of surfing the web and going on the internet. With the internet you can communicate with people abroad face to face on Skype, you can download films and music, you can send messages on social networks and do business.

Disadvantages of computers / internet

L'inconvénient c'est que l'internet présente des dangers pour tout le monde. Le danger principal c'est qu'on peut perdre beaucoup de temps en faisant tout ça, et devenir accro. De plus il y a le risque de vol d'identité et de cyber intimidation sur les réseaux sociaux. Il y a des enfants qui ont été tués par les inconnus qu'ils ont rencontrés en ligne. Et bien que les personnes âgées qui vivent seules, puissent maintenant avoir les moyens de rester en contact avec le monde, la plupart de ces personnes n'ont pas toujours envie d'apprendre comment en profiter car ils le trouvent trop compliqué.

The disadvantage is that the internet presents dangers for everyone. The main danger is that you can waste a lot of time doing all that, and become addicted. There is also the risk of identity theft and online bullying on social networks. There are children who have been killed by strangers they have met online. And although old people living alone can now have the means to stay in contact with the world, most of these people don't always want to learn to make the most of it as they find it too complicated.

The future of mobile phones

A l'avenir, les portables deviendront de plus en plus puissants, minces et légers. Je pense qu'on va probablement les porter comme une montre. Comme ça on pourra les consulter à tout moment et rester en contact avec tout le monde tout le temps sans devoir sortir l'appareil de la poche. C'est un peu effrayant, ne pas pouvoir s'échapper des messages et des demandes de la vie. Je ne veux pas y penser !

In the future, phones will become more powerful, thinner and lighter. I think we will probably be wearing them like watches. Then we will be able to use them at all times and stay in touch with everyone all the time without having to get the device out of our pocket. It's a bit scary, the idea of not being able to escape from messages and the demands of life. I don't want to think about it.

Role play at GCSE

The role play element does not exist yet in Edexcel IGCSE but is super-useful as an exercise if you want to feel confident out and about in a French-speaking country, some would say essential! Other exam boards give you a short time to prepare a role play exercise where you will usually play the role of a student going to stay with a family, or a tourist needing some information. Be prepared to talk about something going wrong, like leaving your bag in the restaurant, your wallet in the taxi, missing planes and losing passports.

The best way to prepare for this is to revise set phrases that often arise, so they are grouped below in subject matter.

Initiating a conversation

Excusez-moi	Excuse me
Je peux vous aider	Can I help you ?
Allo ?	Hello (answering phone)
Salut	Hi / Hey
Bonjour / Bonsoir	Hello (formal)
Je vous appelle parce que	I'm calling you because
J'ai réservé une chambre	I have reserved a room

Directions

Pour aller à la gare ?	How do I get to the station?
Allez tout droit	Go straight on
Jusqu'aux feux	Until the lights
Prenez	Take
La première rue à droite	the first road on the right
La deuxième rue à gauche	the second left

Apologizing

Je suis désolé	I'm sorry
Pardon	Excuse me (bumping into someone)

Lateness and reasons for lateness

Je suis en retard	I'm late
Je vais arriver	I'm going to arrive
Plus tard que j'avais prévu	later than I had planned
Le vol a été annulé	the flight was cancelled
Je me suis disputé avec	I argued with
J'ai raté le train	I missed the train

Losing things

J'ai perdu mon passeport	I have lost my passport
J'ai laissé mon sac dans…	I left my bag in….
J'ai oublié mon portefeuille	I have forgotten my wallet

The role play exercise – asking questions

Questions with a yes or no answer

The role play will require you, amongst other things, to formulate questions. When asking a question to which the answer is yes or no, just say the statement in a questioning voice:

Je dois payer?	Do I have to pay?
On doit sortir?	Do we have to go out?
On peut sortir?	Can we go out?
Tu veux venir?	Do you want to come?
Il va faire beau?	Will the weather be good?

Tu a bien dormi?	Did you sleep well?
C'est ouvert?	Is it open?
C'est fermé?	Is it closed?
C'est loin du camping?	Is it far from the campsite?
C'est près du camping?	Is it near the camp site?

Est-ce que.... Alternative

Alternatively, you can turn those statements into questions as above but insert est-ce que just before it:

Est-ce que c'est près du camping ?	Is it near the campsite?
Est-ce que c'est ouvert ?	Is it open ?
Est-ce qu'on doit payer ?	Do we have to pay?
Est-ce que je peux venir ?	Can I come ?
Est-ce que vous avez une chambre ?	Have you got a room?
Est-ce qu'il va faire beau ?	Will the weather be good?

Questions using question words requiring fuller answers

In other situations, you will need question words like *why, when, where, who* etc. We looked at these in section one but here they are with more examples and in more detail because in the role play you will need to form questions rather than just understand them. Question words are used in questions that require more than just a yes or no answer. On the previous page we were just asking questions that required confirmation *(Is it open? Do we have to go out?)* but here we need more information, such as where something is, why something has happened or when something happened.

First option: question word + est-ce que + statement

Quand *est-ce que* tu pars ?	When do you leave?
Où *est-ce que* tu veux habiter ?	Where do you want to live?
Pourquoi *est-ce qu'*elle est triste ?	Why is she sad?
Est-ce que tu comprends les mots ?	Do you understand the words?
Qu'est-ce que tu fais ?	What are you doing ?

Second option: question word + verb + subject

A quelle heure ouvre le magasin ?	What time does the shop open?
Qui est-il ?	Who is he?
Combien as-tu?	How many do you have?
Comprends-tu les mots	Do you understand the words
Que fais-tu	What are you doing?

Where there is a clash of vowels in two consecutive words, a *t* is required in between:

A quelle heure arrive-t-il ?	When does he arrive?
Où a-t-il mis mon sac ?	Where did he put my bag?
Qu'a-t-elle fait ?	What has she done?
Quand a-t-il déménagé ?	When did he move
Comment voyage-t-elle ?	How is she travelling?

When working out how to ask a question, bear in mind the options above. Below is a list of questions words and phrases, and each one has an alternative structure using *est-ce que* (see first option above). I have just given the second option with each phrase for simplicity's sake, but feel free to adapt as you like according to the rules above.

A quelle heure = *when (at what time)*

A quelle heure part le train ?	When does the train leave?
A quelle heure êtes-vous arrivé ?	When did you arrive?
A quelle heure sors-tu ?	What time are you going out?

Quand = *when (generally)*

Quand est ton anniversaire ?	When is your birthday?
Quand allons-nous manger ?	When are we going to eat?
Quand as-tu vu le film ?	When did you see the film?

Comment = *how / what's it like*

Comment vas-tu au collège ?	How do you go to school?
Comment a-t-il trouvé le film ?	How did he find the film?
Comment est ton frère ?	What's your brother like?

Où = *where*

Où est la gare ?	Where is the station?
Où est le magasin ?	Where is the shop?
Où as-tu mis mon sac ?	Where did you put my bag?

Combien de = *how many*

Combien de frères as-tu ?	How many brothers have you?
C'est pour combien de personnes ?	For how many people is it?
Pour combien de nuits ?	For how many nights?

Pourquoi = *why*

Pourquoi es-tu triste ?	Why are you sad?

Pourquoi a-t-il acheté la voiture ?	Why did he buy the car?
Pourquoi devons-nous retourner ?	Why do we have to go back?

Qui = *who*

Qui as-tu invitè ?	Who have you invited?
Qui allons-nous voir ?	Who are we going to see?
Qui aimes-tu ?	Who do you like?

Que OR Qu'est-ce que = *what*

Qu'est-ce que c'est ?	What is it?
Qu'est-ce que tu penses ? / Que penses-tu ?	What do you think?
Qu'est-ce que tu as fait ? / Qu'as-tu fait ?	What have you done?
Qu'est-ce que tu veux ? / Que veux-tu ?	What do you want?
Qu'est-ce qu'il y a ? Qu'y a-t-il ?	What is there?

Stating preferences

Je voudrais aller au cinéma	I'd like to go to the cinema
Je préfère nager	I prefer swimming
Je n'aime pas les champignons	I don't like mushrooms
J'adore le cinéma	I love the cinema

Understanding instructions in the role play

Whereas the AQA and Edexel role play relates closely to the material in the general conversation, Cambridge IGCSE is slightly different and requires the candidate to understand instructions such as:

Réagissez avec plaisir	react with pleasure
Posez une question	ask a question

Répondez à la question	answer the question
Expliquez la situation	explain the situation
Saluez votre ami	say hello to your friend
Dites ce que vous faites	say what you're doing
Proposez de payer	offer to pay
Expliquez pourquoi	explain why
Demandez le prix	ask the price
Faites vos excuses	apologise
Choisissez un dessert	choose a pudding

Surprise question

The role play will include a surprise question. Have a look at the situation described and try to imagine what might come up. It will probably be an opportunity to use a tense that has not come up yet in the planned questions. Remember you know all this from revision of the general conversation questions and answers.

Top tips for the oral

Use all the tenses

Make sure you have used:

- Present (including irregulars and reflexives) to describe what you normally do
- Passé composé (using etre and avoir and reflexives) to describe events in the past
- Imperfect to describe repeated actions in the past or unfinished action
- Both types of future tense and future used with quand – *quand je serai adulte*...
- Conditional (including combining with imperfect in an *if* sentence)
- (possibly) pluperfect, in conjunction with passé compose to describe what *had* happened
- Past conditional, with pluperfect, to say what you would have done *if*...

Special verb structures

En lisant	while reading
Après avoir mangé	after eating
Avant de sortir	before going out
Je suis en train de	I'm in the middle of
Je viens de	I have just
Sur le point de	about to

Opinions and justifications

Je pense que	I think that
Je trouve que	I find that
Je le trouve facile	I find it easy
A mon avis	In my opinion
Selon moi	according to me
Parce que / car c'est	because it is

Positive opinions on things

Ça vaut la peine	it's worth it
Ça valait la peine	it was worth it
Ça fait du bien	it feels good
Ça me fait plaisir	it makes me happy
Je suis ravi de partir en vacances	I'm excited about my holiday
J'ai hâte d'y retourner	I can't wait to go back there
J'attends .... avec impatience	I am looking forward to ......
On a passé un bon moment	we had a great time
C'est à tomber	it's to die for
Ça me fait rire	it makes me laugh
Je suis fort en maths	I'm good at maths

Negative opinions on things

J'en ai marre	I'm sick of it
J'en ai ras le bol	I've had enough
Ça me fait peur	I'm scared of it
C'est nul	It's rubbish
Je suis nul en maths	I'm rubbish at maths
J'ai horreur de	I have a horror of / hate
Un cauchemar	a nightmare

Avoir expressions

J'ai de la chance	I'm lucky
J'ai envie de	I want to, I feel like
J'ai du mal à	I find it hard to
J'ai hâte de	I'm looking forward to
J'ai besoin de	I need
Tout ce dont j'ai besoin	Everything I need

Comparatives and superlatives

Plus sympa que	nicer than
Moins sportif que	less sporty than

Le film le plus passionnant	the most exciting film
Le meilleur pays du monde	the best country in the world

Y and depuis

J'y habite depuis cinq ans	I've lived there for five years
J'y joue depuis cinq ans	I've been playing for five years
J'ai envie d'y retourner	I'd like to go back there
J'y suis accro	I'm addicted to it
Je n'y suis jamais allé	I've never been there

En

Je m'en sers pour tout	I use it for everything
J'en profite	I make the most of it
Je n'en prends jamais	I never take any (drugs)
J'en mange tous les jours	I eat it (some of it) evey day
Il n'y en a pas	there aren't any (cycle paths)
Il n'y en a pas assez	there aren't enough of them
Je ne pourrais pas m'en passer	I couldn't manage without it

Dont

Il y a tout ce dont j'ai besoin	there is everything I need
Tout ce dont j'ai besoin	everyting I need

Preceding direct / indirect objects

Les profs nous donnent	the teachers give us
Je le trouve ennuyeux	I find it boring
Ça ne le dérange pas	it doesn't bother him
Je lui ai acheté un cadeau	I bought him / her a presesnt

Subjunctive expressions

Pour que je puisse	so that I can
Bien que ce soit	although it is
Quoi que ce soit	whatever it may be

Il faut qu'on fasse des efforts pour	we've got to try to
Avant que ce ne soit trop tard	before it's too late
Je ne pense pas que ce soit	I don't think it is
Sans que leurs parents ne le sachent	without their parents' knowledge

Pour + infinitive

pour regarder un film	to watch a film
pour acheter un cadeau	to buy a present

De with adjectives that come before the noun

De bonnes notes	good marks
De mauvaises notes	bad marks
De bons effets spéciaux	good special effects
Pour de diverses raisons	for a variety of reasons

Impersonal expressions

On peut	one can / you can
On doit	one must / you have to
Il faut	you have to
Il me faut (plus time)	it takes me
Il me faut (plus noun)	I need
Il suffit de	all you have to do is
Il s'agit de	it's about

Modals in all tenses

On doit porter un uniforme	we have to wear uniform
J'ai dû en acheter un autre	I had to buy another
On devrait recycler plus	we should recycle more
J'aurais dû appeler	I should have called
Je ne pouvais pas m'en sortir	I couldn't manage
Il aurait pu faire des efforts	he could have made an effort
Je voudrais apprendre à nager	I would like to learn to swim
Je ne veux pas commencer à fumer	I don't want to start smoking

Negatives

Je ne fume pas	I don't smoke
Je n'ai jamais fume	I have never smoked
Je ne le ferai plus	I won't do it anymore
Personne ne fume	Nobody smokes
Il n'y a aucune raison	There is no reason
Il n'y a rien à faire	There's nothing to do
Il n'y a que des anglais	there are only English people

Ce que

Ce que j'aime le plus c'est	what I like best is
Ce que je n'aime pas, c'est que	what I don't like is

Idioms

J'en ai marre	I'm sick of it
J'en ai ras le bol	I've had enough
Ils ont du mal à se débrouiller	they struggle to get by
Il fait un froid de canard	it's freezing cold
Il pleut des grenouilles	it's pouring
Je n'en ferai pas une rame	I won't lift a finger
coutent les yeux de la tête	cost a bomb
Donner un coup de main à qq	give someone a hand
Scotché à l'écran	glued to the screen
Le suspense m'a tenu en haleine	I was riveted
les yeux plus gros que le ventre	eyes bigger than the stomach
Il n'arrête pas de faire l'andouille	he doesn't stop messing about

PART 3

Writing

Your oral answers will be your first port of call when approaching the writing task. But don't churn them out verbatim – check carefully what the question is asking for first. When approaching the long piece of writing, you should base it on what you know well. Don't use any language you haven't used or practised before unless you absolutely have to.

Describing a place

There are three main places you could end up having to describe: your house, your town or your school, and all of them can follow the same pattern. The idea is to go from a bird's eye view down to the ground. There are seven stages to this piece of writing:

- **Give a general location**
  Il / elle se trouve près de …. dans le nord / sud de l'Angleterre.
  It's near….. in the north / south of England

- **Supply some qualified adjectives**
  C'est assez grand et très animé *It's quite big and very lively*

- **Magic sentence with 5 key phrases**
  1. J'ai de la chance *I'm lucky*
  2. car à mon avis *because in my opinion*
  3. c'est la meilleure région / école / maison du monde
     it's the best region / school / house in the world
  4. et j'y habite / vais
  5. depuis cinq ans
     and I've lived / been going there for 5 years

- **Explain why it's so good there in a sentence**
  Ce que j'aime, c'est qu'il y a tout ce dont j'ai besoin.
  What I like is that there is everything I need.

- **Describe what there is and what one can do there**
  Il y a un…. où on peut   there is a …. where you can

- **A disadvantage**
  Ce que je n'aime pas, c'est qu'il n'y a pas de piscine.
  What I don't like is that there isn't a swimming pool.

- **What you would change**

S'il y avait une piscine, je serais content(e).
If there was a swimming pool, I would be happy.

Example description of school
Mon college s'appelle Thornton High school. Il se trouve près de Liverpool dans le nord-ouest de l'Angleterre.
C'est assez grand, moderne et sympa.
J'ai de la chance car à mon avis c'est le meilleur collège du monde et j'y vais depuis cinq ans.
Ce que j'aime c'est qu'il y a tout ce dont j'ai besoin.
Il y a un terrain de sport où on peut jouer au foot et une bibliothèque où on peut travailler.
Ce que je n'aime pas c'est qu'il n'y a pas de piscine.
S'il y avait une piscine je serais content(e).

Describing an event

You are very likely to have to write about an occasion or event, which will require effective use of the past tense. Here are some sample passages in the past tense which use not only the passé composé but the present, the imperfect, the pluperfect, the conditional and some other impressive structures like:

avant de+ infinitive	before (doing something)
après avoir + past participle	after (doing something)
en + gerund	while / upon (doing something)
y (pronoun)	there (eg. J'y vais – I go there)
j'ai dû rentrer (modal verb)	I had to go home
quel desastre!	What a disaster!
Je *l*'ai aimé (pronoun)	I liked *it*

Read the stories below which use some of the key expressions listed above.

Le week-end dernier mes amis et moi sommes allés en ville pour faire du shopping. Si j'avais plus d'argent **j'irais** plus souvent. J'ai acheté un nouveau T-shirt et des baskets parce que je suis sportif et je joue au foot tous les jours. **Avant de** rentrer chez moi, je suis allé(e) au cinéma pour voir un film d'action. Je l'ai aimé parce qu'il y avait de bons effets spéciaux. Mais, **quelle** catastrophe ! **En arrivant** chez moi j'ai vu que **j'avais perdu** mon porte-monnaie ! Heureusement **j'avais depensé** tout mon argent et **c'etait** vide.

Last weekend my friends and I went into town to go shopping. If I had more money I'd go more often. I bought a new T-shirt and some trainers because I am sporty and I play football every day. Before returning home I went to the cinema to see an action film. I liked it because there were good special effects. But, what a disaster! On arriving home I saw that I had lost my purse! Luckily I had spent all my money and it was empty.

Samedi après-midi ma famille et moi sommes allés à mon restaurant préféré pour fêter l'anniversaire de ma mère. **Avant de** sortir, j'ai fait un joli gâteau d'anniversaire. Au restaurant, j'ai mangé des pâtes avec du fromage parce que je suis végétarienne. Si je pouvais, je **mangerais** des pâtes tous les jours. Ma mère a reçu beaucoup de cadeaux et elle **était** très contente. Mais, **quel** désastre ! Quand nous sommes rentrés le chien **avait mangé** le gâteau. J'étais triste parce que j'adore le gâteau et le chien **était** malade.

On Saturday afternoon my family and I went to my favourite restaurant to celebrate my mother's birthday. I ate pasta with cheese because I am vegetarian. My mother received lots of presents and she was very happy. But, what a disaster! When we came home the dog had eaten the cake! I was sad because I love cake and the dog was ill.

Lundi dernier **j'étais** très content car nous avons fait une visite scolaire au musée des sciences, et la biologie c'est ma matière préférée. Pendant mon temps libre je lis des livres sur les sciences et je regarde des vidéos scientifiques sur YouTube **en mangeant** mon dîner. La visite était très intéressante. **Après avoir visité** le musée nous avons fait un pique-nique dans le parc. Mais **quel** désastre ! Il a plu et nous **avons dû** rentrer au collège très vite. Si je pouvais **j'irais** au musée tous les jours.

Last Monday I was very happy because we went on a school trip to the science museum, and biology is my favourite subject. During my free time I read books on science and I watch scientific videos on YouTube while eating my dinner. The outing was very interesting. After visiting the museum, we had a picnic in the park. But what a disaster! It rained, and we had to hurry back to school. If I could I'd go to the museum every day.

The key expresssions can also be used in the future tense in connection with a planned rather than a completed activity.

Le week-end prochain je vais aller en ville avec mes amis. Nous prendrons le bus car c'est rapide et facile. J'adore ma ville car il y a plein d'activités, mais mon passe-temps préféré c'est le cinéma et **j'y vais** tous les samedis. Si je pouvais, **j'y irais** tous les jours. **Avant de** regarder le film nous allons acheter des bonbons avec notre argent de poche et nous regarderons le film **en mangeant**. Ce sera délicieux. **Après avoir regardé** le film je **devrai** rentrer pour faire mes devoirs.

Next weekend I'm going to go into town with my friends. We will take the bus as it is fast and easy. I love my town as there are lots of activities, but my favourite pastime is the cinema and I go there every Saturday. Before watching the film, we will buy sweets with our pocket money and will watch the film (while) eating. It will be delicious. After having watched the film I will have to go home to do my homework.

Final checking of the writing task

Like the oral, the writing part of the exam is where you are in charge. You can get top marks here and risk losing a few in the harder parts of the listening. Make this work to your advantage. Where the writing exam really helps is in giving you time to consider your answer, check it and amend it, which you don't get to do in the oral.

Use your oral answers

There are plenty of parallels between the oral and the writing exams. This means that once you are familiar with the oral you will be able to use a lot of the material in the writing. My YouTube channel shows you how to remember the standard answers relating to describing a person, place or activity, and gives you the standard technique to answer questions on technology and environment. So when you're learning the oral answers, just remember you're killing two birds with one stone.

Read the question!

Plenty of people get caught out by questions which *appear* to be one of the standard answers but which only require a section of it. For example, part of the question may require you to talk about the advantages OR disadvantages of the internet, so you're wasting your time doing both. The examiner will think you don't know the meaning of the word *or*. If they ask you specifically what you do at home to help protect the environment, don't talk about public transport because that happens away from the house. If they want you to explain the importance of eating healthily, focus on that rather than on the activities side of the health topic. Where you do venture into other areas, keep them linked clearly to the question you are answering.

Choose your question carefully

Don't plump for the question that appears to be on a topic you know well. First you need to check and double check that you understand what each point is that you need to address. You may be an expert on describing your town by now, but is that what they want, or does the question contain vocabulary that you don't know. Even if there is one word in one bullet point that you don't understand, this could lose you 25% of your available marks.

Leave a line

If you write out the bare bones of your answer using alternate lines, there will be room to go back and fill in the gaps when you remember some key expressions you should have used. This may look a bit odd, but much easier to space it out than to have the examiner struggle to navigate asterisks and tiny handwriting squashed into the gaps.

Check, check and check again

Check that subject and verb agree, and that article, noun and adjective agree. In English we can say *They like big houses* without bothering with any of that. In French you will need to agree every word *Ils aiment les grandes maisons.*

Do not attempt to express anything you haven't said before

This is not the time or the place to try out new stuff. Stick to what you know. If you're not sure, go another route.

The AAAA test:

- Agreements (eg ma ville est *belle, mes* amis / *mon* ami, nous sommes allé<u>s</u>, la meilleur<u>e</u> région / maison, ma matière préféré<u>e</u>)
- Apostrophes eg. *parce qu'il*, not *parce que il*
- Accents – passé composé needs acute accents. Use grave accents only in certain cases (see vocab lists at the back)
- Alphabet – see below!

Use my mnemonic

As part of this checking procedure, use this mnemonic, which takes you from L to V in the alphabet. I have listed the letters on the next page, what they stand for, and examples of each.

The writing mnemonic…

Leave a line so you can add things later to increase word count.

Modals

The verbs to have to, to be able to, to want to are all modal verbs and you need to show the examiner that you can use them in all tenses

J'ai dû rentrer chez moi	I had to go home
On devrait protéger l'environnement	We should protect
On peut faire du sport	One can do sport
Je veux être avocat	I want to be a lawyer

Negatives

Je n'ai pas d'animaux	I don't have pets
Je ne fumerais jamais	I would never smoke
Il n'y a plus d'argent	There's no more money

Opinions

A mon avis	In my opinion
Je crois / pense que	I think / believe that
Il me semble que	It seems to me that

Pronouns

Les profs nous donnent	The teachers give us
Je me lève	I get up
Je le trouve facile	I find it easy

Quel

Quel désastre !	What a disaster!
Quelle chance !	What luck

Reasons

Parce que, car, puisque	because

Superlatives (and comparatives)

Le meilleur collège de Londres	The best school in London
Il est plus sportif que moi	He is more sporty than me

Time phrases

Avant de + infinitive	before (doing something)
Après avoir + past participle	After (doing something)
En arrivant	On arriving
Je viens de	I have just
Il est sur le point de	He is about to
Tous les jours	Every day

Umbrella (weather!)

Il a fait chaud / beau	It was hot
Il pleut / il neige	It is raining / snowing
Il pleuvait / il neigeait	It was raining / snowing
Il a plu / il a neigé	It rained / snowed

Verbs

Use all the tenses you can possibly cram in:

Present   eg. Je fais beaucoup de sport

Perfect   eg. Il a fait beau

Imperfect   eg. Quand j'etais jeune

Near Future   eg. Je vais aller au cinéma

Future simple   eg. Nous irons au théâtre

Conditional   eg. J'acheterais une piscine

Present subjunctive   eg. Pour que je puisse nager

PART 4

Reading

Vocabulary

The key to getting a high mark in the reading and the listening is vocabulary. There are vocab lists by topic at the back of this book and you should know all of it by exam day. Yes, all of it.

Word tricks

If you spot a word you recognize, don't jump to conclusions and assume it's the answer to the question you're looking at. Chances are, it's a red herring, so look at the sentence as a whole for meaning and to check there isn't a negative hiding in there which would make the meaning entirely the opposite of what you thought.

Gapfill expectations

When you're doing a gapfill exercise, look carefully at the sentence and work out what kind of word you expect to fill the gap with. If the gap is preceded by an article, it is likely to be a noun, if it's preceded by a noun and followed by a verb, it's likely to be an adjective because adjectives generally come after nouns, but expect in each case for there to be at least a couple of options in the box to choose from. If the options are the same adjective but with different endings, look for clues as to the gender of the word it is describing.

Reading a comprehension

Make sure you spend plenty of time on this exercise. To start with, read the text twice to get a general idea of what it is about. Read through all the questions as they may help too.

Bouncing along

This is about concentrating on what you know rather than on what you don't. Most students understand a lot more of a written passage if they "bounce" from familiar word to familiar word, creating a stepping- stone path, or a join-the-dots map which will usually give a good indication of meaning. Even if you only know every fifth word, you are likely to get some understanding from that approach.

Guessing the meaning of words

There are dozens, maybe even hundreds of cognates in French. These are words that are almost identical to the English. Here are just a few of them

absence (absence)

ballet (ballet)

calculatrice (calculator)

débat (debate)

édition (edition)

festival (festival)

génération (generation)

horreur (horror)

impression (impression)

juin (june)

kilometre (kilometer)

liberté (liberty)

musique (music)

nombre (number)

opéra (opera)

peintre (painter)

qualité (quality)

raison (reason)

statut (status)

transaction (transaction)

univers (universe)

visiteur (visitor)

wagon (wagon)

xylophone (xylophone)

yaourt (yogurt)

zéro (zero)

absolu (absolute)

britannique (british)

catholique (catholic)

dramatique (dramatic)

entier (entire)

fréquent (frequent)

graduel (gradual)

horrible (horrible)

illégal (illegal)

logique (logical)

mental (mental)

nerveux (nervous)

ordinaire (ordinary)

parlementaire (parliamentary)

romantique (romantic)

sincère (sincere)

traditionnel (traditional)

urgent (urgent)

vulnérable (vulnerable)

abandonner (abandon)

bloquer (block)

capturer (capture)

détruire (destroy)

établir (establish)

finir (finish)

gouverner (govern)

identifier (identify)

limiter (limit)

mentionner (mention)

noter (note)

observer (observe)

posséder (possess)

qualifier (qualify)

répondre (respond)

étudier (study)

transformer (transform)

unir (unite)

varier (vary)

False Friends

These may look like cognates, but their real meanings are entirely different:

journée (day, **not** journey)

librairie (bookstore, **not** library)

coin (corner, **not** coin)

monnaie (coin, **not** money)

location (rent, **not** location)

blesser (to hurt, **not** to bless)

pain (bread, **not** pain)

actuellement (now, **not** actually)

éventuellement (possibly, **not** eventually)

déception (disappointment, **not** deception)

attendre (to wait for, **not** to attend)

personne (nobody, **not** always person)

Words within words

Look for words within words such as the word *merci* in *remercier (to thank)* and the word *chaud (hot)* in *chauffage (heating), imprimer (to print)* in the noun *imprimante* (printer).

If a word ends in -aux, could this be a plural of a word ending in -al? (journaux – newspapers, sociaux – social)

Question words and expected answers

A list of the meanings of question words is set out in the Speaking section (part 2) of this book. Here is a reminder:

Quel est .....?	Which is / What is...?
Quels sont...? / Quelles sont....?	Which are / What are...?
Que (eg que manges-tu?)	What (what are you eating?)
A quelle heure ?	When (at what time?)
Quand ?	When (generally)?
Comment ?	How?
Comment est ...?	What is ..... like?
Où ?	Where?
Qui ?	Who?
Pourquoi ?	Why?
Décris / décrivez	Describe
Explique / expliquez	Explain
Raconte / racontez	Tell

However, you are likely to encounter more complex questions structures in the comprehension like:

Depuis combien de temps... – *for how long...* (inviting an answer beginning with *depuis...*)

Comment sait-on que – *how do we know that* (inviting an answer beginning with *parce que...*)

Changing the person

If the passage is in the first person and you are asked a question on it in the third person, you will need to make changes to reflect that rather than just lifting the text. For example, if the text says *Je suis allée au centre commercial,* you will have to change this to *elle est allée au centre commercial.*

Rules for changing person
Change *je* to *il / elle*
Change *nous* to *ils / elles*
Change *mon* to *son*
Change *ma* to *sa*
Change *mes* to *ses*

Lift the right bits

Don't lift too much from the text or you won't get the marks. Only take what is necessary to answer the question to prove that you have done more than just locate the general area of the passage where the answer can be found.

PART 5

Listening

Listening is for most students the hardest part of the exam. The best thing you can do is stay calm and alert. You need to be on top of your vocabulary and be aware in particular of synonyms and homonyms.

Synonyms

There is more than one way of expressing most things. Just take a look at the number of ways you can express *liking* for a start...

Liking and agreement

j'aime	I like
j'adore	I love
ça me plait	it pleases me
ça me fait plaisir	it gives me pleasure
c'est bon	it's good / tasty
je l'aime	I like it
ça fait du bien	it feels good
ça m'a plu	I liked it / it pleased me
agréable	pleasant
intéressant	interesting
passionnant	exciting
ça me passionne	it excites me
ça m'intéresse	it interests me
c'est mon truc	it's my thing
j'y suis accro	I am addicted to it
d'accord	okay, I agree
tu as raison	you are right
je partage ton opinion	I share your opinion
je pense la même chose	I think the same thing

Disliking and disagreement

je déteste	I hate
j'ai horreur de	I hate
j'en ai marre	I'm sick of it
ça m'embête	it annoys me
c'est embêtant	it's annoying
ça m'énerve	it annoys me
c'est énervant	it's annoying
ce n'est pas mon truc	it's not my thing
nul	rubbish
tu as tort	you are wrong
tu n'as pas raison	you are not right
tu dis des bêtises	you are talking rubbish
je ne partage pas ton avis	I don't share your opinion
je pense autrement	I think differently
je suis contre	I am against it

Students

les élèves	pupils
les lycéens	sixthformers
les étudiants	students

A method, manner or way of doing something

une méthode	method
une façon	fashion or means
un moyen	a means
une manière	a manner

To talk

parler de	talk about
discuter de	discuss
bavarder	to chat
tchatter	to chat online
papoter	to chat (familiar)

Jobs

le travail	work
un poste	a post / job
un emploi	a job
un boulot	a job
un métier	a job
une carrière	a career
les ouvriers	workers
les salariés	workers
les syndicats	trade unions
la classe ouvrière	the working classes
le chômage	unemployment
faire la grève	to strike
une société	a company or society
une entreprise	a company / enterprise
renvoyer	to sack
licencier	to sack
manifester	to protest

Prices

bon marché	cheap
cher	expensive
pas cher	not expensive
couteux	costly
moins cher	less expensive
moins couteux	less costly
plus cher	more expensive
plus couteux	more costly
prix bas	low prices
prix élévés	high prices
gratuit	free
payant	not free

Not allowed

on ne peut pas	one cannot
c'est interdit	it is forbidden
ce n'est pas permis	it's not permitted
on ne permet pas	one does not allow
il ne faut pas	one must not
on n'a pas le droit	we can't / we don't have the right

Essential

il faut	it is necessary
on doit	one must
obligatoire	obligatory / compulsory
primordial	essential

essentiel	essential
inéluctable	inevitable
obligé de	obliged to
il n'y a pas de choix	there is no choice

Food

la nourriture	food
les aliments	food items
l'alimentation	food
la cuisine	cuisine / food
un repas	a meal
un plat	a dish

how often ?

toujours	always
sans exception	without exception
dans tous les cas	in every case
sans arrêter	without stopping
souvent	often
de temps en temps	sometimes
parfois	sometimes
sauf le jeudi	except on Thursdays
presque toujours	nearly always

To keep healthy

rester en forme	to stay healthy
garder la forme	to keep fit

avoir une bonne santé	to be in good health
suivre un régime	to be on a diet
manger sain(ement)	to eat healthily
éviter	to avoid

To move

bouger	to move (generally)
se déplacer	to move around (by any means)
circuler	to move around (transport)
déménager	to move house

Funny

drôle	funny
marrant	funny
amusant	fun
rigolo	funny (from rigoler – to giggle)
il me fait rire	it makes me laugh
sourire	to smile

Teaching

le / la prof	teacher
une maitresse	teacher (mistress)
un instituteur	teacher (man)
une institutrice	teacher (woman)
l'enseignant(e)	teacher (general)
enseigner	to teach
apprendre	to learn or teach

Homonyms

Some words have the same sound but different meanings. You will need to work out the meaning from the context. Here are some examples of typical homonyms (or words that can sound very similar) that can really confuse students in listening exams.

vent (wind)	vend (sells)	
voit (sees)	voix (voice)	
verre (glass)	vert (green)	vers (towards)
pois (peas)	poids (weight)	
dos (back)	d'eau (of water)	
dans (in)	dent (tooth)	
moi (me)	mois (month)	
toi (you)	toit (roof)	
cette (this)	sept (seven)	
tente (tent)	tante (aunt)	
pris (taken)	prix (prize or price)	
ça (it)	sa (his or her)	
plus (more)	plu (pleased)	plu (rained)
plus tôt (earlier)	plutôt (rather)	
bois (wood)	bois, boit (drink)	
doigt (finger)	dois, doit (must)	
lit (bed)	lis, lit (read)	
marché (market)	marcher (to walk)	
mais (but)	mes (my)	
thé (tea)	tes (your)	
cru (raw)	cru (believed)	
mal (badly)	male (male)	
été (summer)	été (been)	

Listen out for added consonants

Sometimes you will have trouble identifying a word because it has an extra consonant on the front. This happens when a clash of vowels has required the previous word (je, de, le, me, que etc) to replace its last vowel with an apostrophe. If you saw it written, it wouldn't cause a problem. But on listening you can easily miss it. The shorter the word the more confusing it is. For example:

L'Inde est belle – India is beautiful

Une pièce *d'or* – a gold coin

Près *d'eux* – near them

J'ai besoin *d'air* – I need air

Je n'ai pas *d'eau* – I don't have any water

Je n'ai *qu'un* frère – I only have one brother

Ça *m'aide* à me relaxer – It helps me relax

Get some practice

Make sure you listen to plenty of recordings from past papers. These are all available online and listening to material from other exam boards will be just as useful. When listening at home, make the most of the chance to listen as many times as you want. This will make you more accustomed to the language and train your ear to pick things up more effectively. Listen to French radio stations such as France Inter, visit www.newsinslowfrench.com and watch French-speaking films, even with subtitles. Read the transcript before you listen to the tape. It will make so much more sense if you have seen the text first.

Look at past question papers

Look at past question papers from your exam board and make yourself familiar with the different types of task and any instructions in French. Different boards have different types of question, from multiple choice to gap-fills, to full French sentences in response to questions on a text.

Good exam technique

Don't panic! Everyone will find this paper the hardest part of the exam. Here are a few tips to help you keep calm:

- Trust your memory. When you listen to someone tell you what they did at the weekend, you can remember it afterwards without taking notes. Try and get used to doing the same here. If you are writing and listening at the same time, you are likely to miss something. Make very brief notes and abbreviate everything.

- Take every chance you get to read the question in advance so you know the exact information to listen out for. You are not expected to understand every word and there will be plenty of language that is irrelevant to the question you need to answer.

- Listen to the end of each passage. If you rush into answering before the speaker has finished, you may miss the crucial twist, such as she likes history, *but she really loves* geography. Pay special attention to negatives, including words like "peu de" which means *few*, rather than *a few*, so the emphasis is on the fact that there are not very many.

- Listen out for tenses. Has she got a dog now or did she have one when she was younger? Is she studying law or is she planning to in the future? Key words could be *actuellement, maintenant* (now) or *aujourd'hui* (today)

- Use your knowledge of France and French-speaking countries. Past exams have included references to *une malienne* which you will be expected to know is a female resident of Mali. Look at the list of "very French things" at the back of this book. Abbreviations such as TGV and SDF should be familiar to you.

- As well as the actual words being spoken, the tone of someone's voice may be helpful in showing their mood. The intonation of someone's voice may tell you if they are making a statement or asking a question

PART 6

Vocabulary lists by topic

With memory techniques

RELATIONSHIPS AND DESCRIBING PEOPLE

Family

dans ma famille	in my family
nous sommes quatre	there are 4 of us
mon père	my father
ma mère	my mother
mes parents	my parents
ainé / cadet	older / younger (m)
ainée / cadette	older / younger (f)
mes grands parents	my grandparents
mon cousin / ma cousine	my cousin
mon oncle	my uncle
ma tante	my aunt
Je suis enfant unique	I'm an only child
mon demi-frère	my half or step-brother
ma demi-sœur	my half or step-sister
mon beau-père	my father-in-law or step
ma belle-mère	my mother-in-law or step
le bébé	baby
le mari	husband
la femme	wife / woman
le garçon	boy
Mon frère s'appelle	my brother is called
Je n'ai **pas de** sœur	I don't have a sister

Top tip: s'appelle = is called, **qui s'appelle** = who is called

J'ai un frère qui s'appelle Charlie= I have a brother called

Mon frère s'appelle Charlie = my brother is called Charlie

How you get on – *use "on"!*

on s'entend bien	we get on well
beaucoup en commun	lots in common
on aime	we like
les mêmes choses	the same things
on se dispute	we argue
la même musique	the same music

Adjectives to describe people

Je suis	I am
Il / elle est	he / she is
grand(e)	tall
petit(e)	small
gros(se)	fat
mince	thin
intéressant(e)	interesting
ennuyeux/-euse	boring
sympa	nice
embêtant(e)	annoying
vieux (vieille)	old
jeune	young
sportif/-ive	sporty
paresseux/-euse	lazy
gentil (gentille)	kind
égoïste	selfish
beau (belle)	beautiful
joli(e)	pretty

laid(e)	ugly
fort(e)	strong
faible	weak
méchant(e)	naughty
agréable	pleasant
désagréable	unpleasant
bavard(e)	chatty
silencieux /-ieuse	silent
marrant(e)	funny
sérieux/-euse	serious
poli(e)	polite
impoli(e)	impolite
triste	sad
fâché(e)	angry
heureux/-euse	happy
sensible	sensitive
de bonne humeur	in a good mood
de mauvaise humeur	in a bad mood
fatigué	tired
énergique	energetic
prudent(e)	careful
maladroit(e)	clumsy
facile à vivre	easygoing
difficile	fussy

Hair adjectives

longs / courts	long / short
raides	straight
frisés / bouclés	curly
blonds / roux / marron	blonde / red / brown
J'ai les cheveux raides	I have straight hair
Il a les cheveux marron *(no s!)*	he has brown hair
Il est chauve	he is bald

General appearance

Il porte des lunettes	he wears glasses
une barbe	beard
une moustache	moustache
Je ressemble à	I look like
On se ressemble	we look similar

General adjectives

plein(e)	full
vide	empty
sain(e)	healthy
malsain	unhealthy
facile	easy
difficile	difficult
chaud(e)	hot
froid(e)	cold
moderne	modern

ancien (-ienne)	old
individuel(le)	detached
jumelé(e)	semi-detached
cher (chère)	expensive
bon marché	cheap
payant(e)	paying (not free)
gratuit(e)	free
sec (sèche)	dry
mouillé(e)	wet
léger (légère)	light
lourd(e)	heavy
lent(e)	slow
rapide	fast
génial(e)	great
pénible	awful
sale	dirty
propre	clean
nouveau (nouvelle)	new
étroit(e)	narrow
large	wide

Example

Mon amie s'appelle Daisy et elle a 15 ans. Elle a les yeux bleus et les cheveux blonds. Elle est très intelligente mais un peu timide et elle est plus sportive que moi. Normalement on s'entend bien parce que nous avons beaucoup de choses en commun mais quelquefois on se dispute car elle n'aime pas ma musique.

Types of relationship and family

toutes sortes de familles	all sorts of families
de bons rapports	good relations
une relation	a relationship
draguer	to chat up
petit copain	boyfriend
petite copine	girlfriend
un rendez-vous	a date
sortir avec	to go out with
tomber amoureux	to fall in love
l'amour	love
rencontrer	to meet
un couple	a couple
fidèle	faithful
ensemble	together (musical)
cohabiter	to live together
avant de se marier	before getting married
se marier avec	to marry
épouser	to marry
se séparer	to separate
divorcer	to get divorced
divorcé	divorced
marié	married
séparé	separated
une famille nombreuse	a big family
une famille recomposée	a blended family
une famille monoparentale	a single parent family
le mariage gay	gay marriage

se disputer	to argue
plaquer	to dump (someone)
la valeur	value
la stabilité	stability
élever un enfant	to bring up a child
adopter	to adopt

HOME

Top tip: Mum owns the house, car, road, the whole town…

Notice that all the rooms in the house, and a lot of the things around the house are **feminine** (house, door, window, car, shelves, wardrobe, TV). Imagine that the only place Dad is allowed is office and sitting room – and garden. He can also have a bed, a computer, a pen and a few other bits (see second list below) but he has to do the housework (le ménage).

Feminine words

une maison individuelle	a detached house
une maison jumelé	a semi-detached house
une maison mitoyenne	a terraced house
une cuisine	a kitchen
une salle à manger	a dining room
une salle de bains	a bathroom
une chambre	a bedroom
une véranda	a conservatory
une voiture	a car
une table	a table

une armoire	a wardrobe *(for your armour)*
une étagère	a bookshelf *(étages - floors)*
une chaise	a chair
une porte	a door
une fenêtre	a window
une lampe	a lamp
une commode	a chest of drawers
une piscine	a swimming pool
une machine à laver	a washing machine
une cuisinière	a cooker
une télévision	a TV
une Xbox / Playstation	Xbox / Playstation
une ville	a town
une rue	a road

Picture Dad in these rooms only

un salon	a sitting room
un jardin	a garden
un grenier	an attic
un bureau	an office

He can sit on

un canapé	a sofa
un fauteuil	an armchair
un lit	a bed

For entertainment he can have

un livre	a book
un ordinateur	a computer
un crayon	a pencil
un stylo	a pen
un portable	a phone
un lave-vaisselle	a dishwasher

Top tip: Describing where things are in the house

*Imagine you're walking round a new house, you keep discovering new floors "Oh! First floor!" "Oh! Second floor!) In French this is "**au** premier étage" and "**au** deuxième étage"*

Daily routine

Je me réveille	I wake up
Je me lève	I get up
Je me douche	I shower
Je me brosse les dents	I brush my teeth
Je m'habille	I get dressed
Je descends	I go downstairs
Je prends mon petit déjeuner	I have my breakfast
Je vais au collège	I go to school
Je rentre chez moi	I go home
Je fais mes devoirs	I do my homework
en regardant la télé	while watching TV

Weekend routine differences

Je fais la grasse matinée	I have a lie-in
Je sors avec mes amis	I go out with my friends
Je me détends	I relax
Je ne fais rien	I do nothing
Je passe la journée au lit	I spend the day in bed

Jobs around the house

pour gagner	in order to earn
mon argent de poche	my pocket money
Je passe l'aspirateur	I vacuum
Je fais la vaisselle	I wash up *(think: vessels)*
Je lave la voiture	I wash the car *(think : lather)*
Je range ma chambre	I tidy my room
Je prépare le diner	I make dinner
Je mets la table	I lay the table *(think : meh)*
Je débarrasse la table	I clear the table
Je sors les poubelles	I take the rubbish out

Not helping at home

Je ne fais rien	I don't do anything
Je n'ai pas le temps	I don't have time
Ils nous donnent	they give us
trop de devoirs	too much homework
plus important	more important
mon brevet	GCSE equivalent
Je suis en train de	I'm in the middle of

Example

Il faut que je fasse des tâches ménagères afin de gagner mon argent de poche, et je pense qu'il est important d'aider avec le ménage, donc je range ma chambre et je mets la table tous les jours. Mais les profs nous donnent trop de devoirs et en ce moment je suis en train de préparer mon brevet, donc je ne fais pas beaucoup.

TOWN

Describing your town

ma ville	my town
mon village	my village
ma région	my region
mon quartier	my neighbourhood
j'y habite depuis 5 ans	I've lived there 5 years
la meilleure région	the best region
à mon avis	in my opinion
ce que j'aime	what I like
c'est qu'il y a	is that there is
tout ce dont j'ai besoin	everything I need
où on peut	where one can
Je vais **au**	I go to the *(masc nouns)*
Je suis allé **au**	I went to the *(masc nouns)*
Je vais **à la**	I go to the *(fem nouns)*
Je suis allé **à la**	I went to the *(fem nouns)*

Example

Ma ville s'appelle Wimbledon. C'est grand, moderne et sympa. J'ai de la chance car à mon avis c'est la meilleure région de Londres et j'y habite depuis cinq ans. Ce que j'aime c'est qu'il y a beaucoup de choses à faire – un cinéma ou on peut regarder des films et un centre commercial ou on peut faire du shopping. Ce que je n'aime pas, c'est la pollution. Si je pouvais changer quelque chose je voudrais avoir moins de circulation.

Masculine places in the town – take "au" and they mostly sound English

le cinéma (je vais **au** cinéma)	cinema
le restaurant	restaurant
le collège	school
le parc	park
le café	cafe
le centre commercial	shopping centre
le centre sportif	sports centre
le coiffeur	hairdresser *(quiff)*
le supermarché	supermarket

Top tip: Feminine places in town – think holiday: go to the bank for money, the library for books, the station to get the train, to the pool, beach, ice rink, then post office to send a postcard.

la banque (je vais **à la** banque)	bank
la bibliothèque	library
la gare	station
la piscine	pool

la plage	beach
la patinoire	ice rink
la poste	post office

> If they begin with a vowel, use **à l'**
>
> Je vais / je suis allé **à l'**école / église / hypermarché
>
> *I go / I went to school, to church, to the hypermarket*

Transport

*All transport that has an **en**gine uses "en"*

en voiture	by car
en avion	by plane
en bus	by bus
en bateau	by boat
en car	by coach
à pied / à vélo	on foot / by bike

On foot and bike, your legs hurt – ah!

Directions

tout droit	straight on
à droite	right
à gauche	left
aux feux	at the traffic lights
en face de	opposite
à côté de	next to
près de	near
devant	in front of
derrière	behind

Shopping

les magasins	the shops
faire les magasins	to go shopping
faire du shopping	to go shopping
faire les courses	to go food shopping
faire des achats	to buy things
acheter	to buy
en ligne	online
le vendeur	shop assistant (male)
la vendeuse	shop assistant (female)
l'argent de poche	pocket money
économiser	to save
dépenser	to spend
gaspiller	to waste
un portefeuille	wallet
les soldes	the sales
faire du lèche vitrine	to go window shopping

Trains

le guichet	ticket office
un billet simple	a single ticket
un billet aller-retour	a return ticket
c'est quel quai?	Which platform is it?
le consigne de bagages	left luggage
rater le train	to miss the train
en retard	late
les bagages	luggage
le voyage	journey

Road accidents

il y a eu un accident	there's been an accident
j'ai eu un accident	I've had an accident
un accident de route	a road accident
un pneu crevé	a flat tyre
un accident	an accident
un embouteillage	a traffic jam
en panne	broken down
le moteur	the engine
les phares	the headlights
l'autoroute	motorway
les urgences	the emergency services
les pompiers	the fire brigade
une ambulance	ambulance
un gendarmes	policeman
un policier	policeman
heurter	to hit, crash into *(hurt!)*
le frein	brake
freiner	to brake
faire le plein	fill up with petrol
l'essence	petrol
la ceinture de sécurité	seat belt
la vitesse	speed
un amende	a fine
un témoin	a witness
le témoignage	testimony
blessé	injured
malade	ill

se casser la jambe	to break one's leg
se casser le bras	to break one's arm
je me suis cassé le bras	I broke my arm
j'ai eu un choc	I had a shock

EDUCATION AND EMPLOYMENT

School subjects

J'étudie	I study
l'histoire	history
l'informatique	ICT
l'anglais	English
les maths	maths
les sciences	science
le sport	sport
le dessin	art
le français	French
la géographie	geography
la musique	music
l'EPS	PE
ma matière préférée	my favourite subject
Je suis fort(e) en	I'm good at
Je suis nul(le) en	I'm bad at
J'ai de bonnes notes	I get good marks
J'ai de mauvaises notes	I get bad marks
Si je pouvais	if I could
je supprimerais les maths	I'd get rid of maths

The school facilities and routine

dans mon collège	in my school
des salles de classe	classrooms
des laboratoires	laboratories
des terrains de sport	sports fields
une bibliothèque	a library
une cantine	a canteen
une piscine	a pool
la cour	the playground
des contrôles	tests
des examens	exams
un théâtre	theatre
en arrivant	on arriving
un cours	lesson
l'uniforme	the uniform
beaucoup de choses à faire	lots of things to do
j'y vais depuis …	I've been going there for…

Example

Mon collège s'appelle …. C'est grand, moderne et sympa. Il y a cent profs et sept cents élèves. J'ai de la chance car à mon avis c'est le meilleur collège de Londres et j'y vais depuis cinq ans. Ce que j'aime c'est qu'il y a beaucoup de choses à faire – une bibliothèque ou on peut lire, une cantine ou on peut manger et un terrain de sport ou on peut jouer au netball. Ce que je n'aime pas, c'est l'uniforme car c'est moche. Si je pouvais changer quelque chose je changerais l'uniforme.

Routine

neuf cours par jour	9 lessons a day
chaque cours dure	each lesson lasts
pendant la récréation	during break time
la pause déjeuner	lunch break
les cours devraient	lessons should
commencer plus tard	begin later
les cours finissent	lessons finish
les activités extra-scolaires	after-school clubs
un voyage scolaire	school trip
un échange	an exchange
interne	a boarder
préparer le brevet	to do your GCSEs

Example

Je vais au collège en bus et j'arrive à huit heures et je bavarde avec mes amis avant les cours. Les cours commencent à neuf heures. Nous avons six cours par jour et chaque cours dure une heure. Pendant la pause je joue avec mes amis et je mange un sandwich. Après avoir mangé je vais au club de netball parce que je suis sportive et c'est très amusant. Les cours finissent à trois heures et je rentre chez moi. Puis je fais mes devoirs avant de manger et après avoir mangé je regarde la télé.

School rules

il faut	you have to
obligatoire	compulsory
on peut	one can
facultatif	optional

on ne peut pas	one cannot
avoir le droit de	to be allowed to
on n'a pas le droit de	we're not allowed to
porter des bijoux	to wear jewellery
utiliser les portables	to use mobiles
parler en classe	to talk in lessons
sécher les cours	to bunk off lessons
J'en ai marre	I'm sick of it
J'en ai ras le bol	I've had enough

After leaving school

Je travaille dur	I work hard
pour que je puisse	so that I can
trouver un bon travail	find a good job
le chômage	unemployment
travailler	to work
faire un stage en entreprise	do work experience
Il travaille comme	he works as a
un boulot, un métier	job
bien payé	well-paid
à plein temps	full-time
à temps partiel	part-time
un travail temporaire	a temporary job
un travail permanent	a permanent job
il faut poser sa candidature	you have to apply
gagner un bon salaire	earn a good salary
beaucoup de chômage	high unemployment
un vendeur / une vendeuse	salesperson

un / une professeur	teacher
un chauffeur	driver
un facteur	postman *(factory of letters)*
un médecin	doctor *(medicine)*
un pharmacien	chemist
un chirurgien	surgeon *(shurgeon)*
un comptable	accountant
un avocat / une avocate	lawyer *(advocate)*
un informaticien /-ienne	IT consultant
un / une secrétaire	secretary
un serveur / une serveuse	waiter
un ingénieur	engineer
un pompier	fireman *(pumps)*
un plombier	plumber *(pb= lead)*
un gendarme	policeman
un infirmier / une infirmière	nurse *(infirmary)*
un coiffeur / -euse	hairdresser *(quiff)*
un photographe	photographer
un commerçant	shopkeeper
un ouvrier / une ouvrière	worker
un homme d'affaires	businessman

Example

L'année prochaine je vais continuer avec la géographie et les maths parce que c'est facile et amusant mais je vais abandonner l'anglais car c'est ennuyeux. Après avoir quitté le collège, je voudrais aller à l'université pour étudier la géo car c'est ma matière préférée. Je pense qu'il est important d'aller à l'université parce que c'est difficile de trouver un emploi sans diplôme.

LEISURE AND HOLIDAYS

Playing games

jouer au foot, rugby, cricket	to play football etc
jouer aux échecs	to play chess
jouer aux cartes	to play cards
jouer à l'ordinateur	to play on computer
jouer à la Xbox	to play Xbox

Playing instruments

jouer du piano	to play piano
jouer du violon	to play violin
jouer de la guitare	to play guitar
jouer de la clarinette	to play clarinet
jouer de la batterie	to play drums

Activities - masculine

faire du sport	to do sport
faire du patinage	to go skating
faire du vélo / cyclisme	to go cycling
faire du VTT	mountain biking
faire du shopping	to go shopping
faire du skate	to skateboard
faire du ski	to go skiing
faire du ski-nautique	to go waterskiing
faire du jardinage	to do gardening
faire du bricolage	to do DIY
faire du camping	to go camping

Activities - feminine

faire de la natation	to go swimming
faire de la voile	sailing
faire de la planche à voile	windsurfing *(plank sail)*
faire de la plongée	diving *(plunge)*
faire de la gymnastique	gymnastics
faire de la danse	dance
faire de la musculation	weight training

and if it begins with a vowel "faire de l'"

faire de l'équitation	to go horseriding
faire de l'athlétisme	athletics
faire de l'escrime	fencing *(scream!)*
faire de l'escalade	climbing *(escalator)*
faire de l'alpinisme	mountaineering *(alps)*

and if it's plural "faire des"

faire des promenades	to go for walks
faire des randonnées	to go hiking

Other hobbies

J'aime la lecture	I like reading
lire	to read
aller à la pêche	to go fishing
faire du camping	go camping
collectionner	to collect
des timbres	stamps
dessiner	to draw
chanter	to sing
danser	to dance
tricoter	to knit
les loisirs	leisure activities
le centre de loisirs	leisure centre

Cinema and TV

le dernier film que j'ai vu	the last film I saw
il s'agit de	it's about
je l'aime	I like it
je l'ai aimé	I liked it
ça me fait rire	it makes me laugh
passionnant	exciting
mon émission préférée	my favourite show
je le trouve	I find it
les dessins animés	cartoons
les actualités / les infos	the news
quotidien	daily
hebdomadaire	weekly
les feuilletons	soaps

les documentaires	documentaries
la téléréalité	reality TV
les jeux télévisés	game shows
la chaine	channel
l'écran	screen
les téléspectateurs	viewers
les auditeurs	listeners
les vedettes	film stars
la zapette	the remote control
les films romantiques	romantic films
les films d'action	action films
les films d'horreur	horror films
les films de guerre	war films
les films de science-fiction	sci fi films
les films d'aventures	adventure films
les films policiers	detective filims

On holiday– en vacances

je suis allé	I went
j'ai passé	I spent (time)
quinze jours	a fortnight
au bord de la mer	by the sea
au camping	at the campsite
en montagne	in the mountains
en colonie de vacances	on a holiday camp
en ville	in the city
nous avons logé	we stayed
dans un hôtel	in a hotel

dans une auberge	at a hostel
dans un appartement	in an apartment
dans une gite	in a gite
à la station balnéaire	at the holiday resort
à la station de ski	at the ski resort
louer	to hire
nous avons loué	we hired
les valises	suitcases
à l'étranger	abroad
j'ai perdu mon passeport	I lost my passport
retardé	delayed
le vol	the flight
a été annulé	was cancelled
J'ai raté l'avion	I missed the plane
il y avait du monde	it was crowded
avec vue sur	with a view over
avec balcon	with a balcony
faire les valises	to pack suitcases
défaire les valises	to unpack
se bronzer	to sunbathe
se détendre	to relax
se reposer	to rest
se baigner	to swim
se souvenir de	to remember
visiter des monuments	to visit monuments
visiter des musées	to visit the museums
prendre des photos	to take photos
goûter les plats régionaux	to sample local dishes

acheter des cadeaux	to buy presents
se faire des amis	to make friends
les sites touristiques	tourist attractions
Il a fait beau	the weather was good
Il a plu deux fois	it rained twice
une canicule	a heatwave
J'ai envie d'y retourner	I'd like to go back there
J'ai hâte d'y aller	I can't wait to go there
le meilleur pays	the best country
J'ai eu de la chance	I was lucky

Example

L'année dernière je suis allé en France en avion avec ma famille. Nous sommes restés dans un hôtel près de la plage pendant quinze jours. Je suis allé à la plage, j'ai joué au tennis avec mon frère, nous avons visité des monuments, j'ai pris des photos et j'ai acheté des cadeaux. J'ai gouté les plats régionaux comme les escargots. Malheureusement, quand c'était l'heure du départ, j'ai perdu mon passeport et nous avons presque raté l'avion. Heureusement je l'ai trouvé dans ma valise.

Je pense que les vacances sont importantes pour beaucoup de raisons :

- On peut essayer une nouvelle activité
- On peut se relaxer
- On peut apprendre une nouvelle langue
- On peut visiter un autre pays

TECHNOLOGY

mon portable	my mobile
mon ordinateur	my computer
je m'en sers pour	I use it to
je l'utilise pour	I use it to
envoyer des messages	to send messages
télécharger de la musique	to download music
accéder à l'internet	to go on the internet
rester à la page	to stay up to date
mettre à jour	to update
mon profil Facebook	my Facebook profile
rester en contact	to stay in touch
j'y suis accro	I'm addicted to it
scotché à l'écran	glued to the screen
je ne pourrais pas m'en passer	I couldn't do without it
le cyber-intimidation	cyber-bullying
les inconnus	strangers
le vol d'identité	identity theft
les sites de rencontre	chat rooms
les réseaux sociaux	social networks
rencontrer en ligne	to meet online
une tablette	tablet
un logiciel malveillant	malware
le piratage	hacking
en conduisant	while driving
en traversant la rue	while crossing the road
on peut avoir un accident	you can have an accident

Example

La technologie est importante pour beaucoup de raisons.

On peut

- rester en contact avec ses amis sur les réseaux sociaux
- envoyer des textos et des mails
- télécharger des films et de la musique et
- jouer sur les applis.

Cependant il y a beaucoup de dangers. Par exemple il y a le risque de cyber-harcèlement / cyber-intimidation, de piratage et de vol d'identité. Si on traverse la rue en regardant l'écran on peut facilement avoir un accident.

A l'avenir je pense que les portables seront plus petits et plus rapides et il y aura des robots dans les maisons pour faire le ménage et dans les collèges pour donner les cours.

ENVIRONMENT AND SOCIAL PROBLEMS

Top tip: The three big environment issues **rhyme**

Les gaz d'echappement causent….

la pollution de l'air	air pollution
le réchauffement de la terre	global warming
l'effet de serre	greenhouse effect

le changement climatique	climate change
la déforestation	deforestation
la pluie acide	acid rain
les tremblements de terre	earthquakes

l'énergie nucléaire	nuclear energy
les ressources naturelles	natural resources
en danger	in danger
les espaces verts	green spaces
la circulation	traffic
les embouteillages	traffic jams
les camions	lorries
les usines	factories
la sécheresse	drought
les inondations	floods (inundated)
les incendies	fires
les ordures / déchets	rubbish
la déchetterie	the tip
les poubelles	bins
le déboisement	deforestation

Top tip: Imagine having a shower, then turning the light off, going down and putting out the recycling, getting on the bus and going shopping for green products…

Je me douche	I shower
Je ferme les robinets	I turn the taps off
pour économiser de l'eau	to save water
J'éteins les lumières	I turn off the lights
Je recycle les emballages	I recycle packaging

J'utilise	I use
les transports en commun	public transport
J'achète des produits bio	I buy organic products
des produits écologiques	green products
on doit / il faut	we must
continuer à	to carry on
J'essaie de	I try to
Je fais des efforts pour	I make an effort to
protéger	to protect
éteindre	to switch off
fermer les robinets	to turn off the taps
économiser	to save
recycler	to recycle
trier	to sort out
les emballages	packaging
le verre	glass
le plastique	plastic
le carton	cardboard
utiliser	to use
acheter	to buy
éviter	to avoid
voyager	to travel
manifester contre	to protest against

Example

Le plus grand problème c'est la pollution. Les voitures et les usines produisent des gaz toxiques qui causent le réchauffement de la planète et l'effet de serre.

Pour protéger la planète :

- Je me douche pour économiser de l'eau (je me suis douché)
- J'éteins les lumières quand je quitte une pièce (j'ai éteint)
- Je recycle le verre, le plastique et le papier (j'ai recyclé)
- J'utilise les transports en commun (j'ai utilisé)
- J'achète des produits écologiques (j'ai acheté)

Social issues

la pauvreté	poverty
la faim	hunger
le terrorisme	terrorism
l'immigration	immigration
accueillir	to welcome
le racisme	racism
le chômage	unemployment
le taux	the rate
est en hausse	is going up
le manque de	the lack of
l'obésité	obesity
la malbouffe	junk food
les sans-abris	the homeless
less SDF (sans domicile fixe)	the homeless

Il faut qu'on fasse	we must do
quelque chose	something
quelque chose d'utile	something useful
pour les aider	to help them
les défavorisés	the less fortunate
le travail bénévole	voluntary work
les organisations caritatives	charities
les bénévoles	charity workers
consacrer du temps	to devote time
collecter de l'argent	to raise money
sensibiliser	to make aware

Example

Il y a un grand problème de pauvreté et de chômage en Angleterre. Il y a beaucoup de sans-abris et c'est très triste quand on voit les gens qui dorment dans la rue. Si j'avais plus de temps libre, j'aiderais dans un abri pour les SDF. Je pense que c'est très important de faire du bénévolat. Ma cousine travaille dans un magasin de Oxfam une fois par semaine. J'aimerais faire du bénévolat aussi mais en ce moment les profs nous donnent trop de devoirs car il y a les examens et je ne peux pas.

WEATHER

il fait beau	the weather is good
il fait mauvais	the weather is bad
il fait chaud	it's hot
il fait froid	it's cold

*With things you can see or feel, say **il y a** = there is*

il y a du vent	it's windy
il y a du soleil	it's sunny
il y a des nuages	it's cloudy
il y a du brouillard	it's foggy
il y a de la brume	it's misty

And if things are falling out of the sky, use the verb!

il neige	it's snowing
il grêle	it's hailing
il pleut	it's raining

But watch out for irregularities with pleuvoir

il a plu	it rained
il va pleuvoir	it is going to rain
la pluie	rain

More weather terms

il fait un froid de canard	it's freezing
il pleut à verse	it's pouring
des averses	showers
le ciel est couvert	it is overcast *(covered)*
la météo	weather forecast
la chaleur	heat *(from chaud)*

la canicule	heatwave
le tonnerre	thunder (*a tonne in the air*)
un orage	storm *(rage)*
une tempête	storm
un éclair	flash of lightning
des éclaircies	sunny spells
frappé par la foudre	struck by lightning
une nuit fraiche	a cold night

FOOD, HEALTH AND BODY

Top tip: The food I ate today is un, une, du de la or des

Un / une – if you eat / drink / want the whole thing

Most fruit is feminine, so imagine ladies eating fruit

une poire	pear
une pomme	apple
une banane	banana
une pêche	peach
une orange	orange
une mandarine	satsuma
une mangue	mango
une pastèque	watermelon
une cerise	cherry
une fraise	strawberry
une framboise	raspberry

| une prune | plum |

Except

un ananas	a pineapple
un melon	a melon
un pamplemousse	a grapefruit
un abricot	an apricot

Remember that if you eat fruit in the plural, use *des*

| Je mange des framboises | I eat raspberries |

Steak with salad, followed by tart with ice cream and a cold drink is FOR LADIES!

une salade	salad
une entrecôte	a steak
une tarte	a tart
une glace	an ice cream
une boisson	a drink
une limonade	a lemonade
une bière	a beer

Stodgy food, spirits and hot drinks FOR MEN!

un œuf	an egg
un croissant	a croissant
un pain au chocolat/raisin	a pastry
un biscuit	a biscuit
un gâteau	a cake
un sandwich	a sandwich

un chocolat chaud	a hot chocolate
un café	a coffee
un thé	a tea
un whisky	a whisky
(except **un** jus d'orange	an orange juce)

Du - with masculine foods – think PICNIC

du pain	bread
du vin	wine
du boursin	(a type of french cheese)
du beurre	butter (bu- - er)
du fromage	cheese
du poulet	chicken
du jambon	ham
du canard	duck
du saucisson	sausage
du salami	salami
du bœuf	beef
du porc	pork
du poisson	fish
du thon	tuna
du cabillaud	cod
du pâté	pâté
du gâteau	cake
du chocolat	chocolate
du sel	salt
du miel	honey
du sucre	sugar

du lait	milk

"De la" - feminine foods are on the RED LIST

de la viande	meat *(red meat)*
de la confiture	jam *(strawberry jam)*
de la glace	ice cream *(strawberry)*
de la pizza	pizza *(tomato pizza)*
de la soupe	soup *(tomato soup)*
de la sauce	sauce *(tomato sauce)*

"De l' if there is some of it and it starts with a vowel

de l'agneau	lamb
de l'eau	water

Plural food – if you eat / have lots, use « des »

des chips	crisps *(not chips !!!!)*
des frites	chips *(fries!)*
des escargots	snails
des céréales	cereal *(plural cereals)*
des pâtes	pasta *(plural pastas)*
des œufs	eggs
des légumes	vegetables
des pommes de terre	potatoes
des carottes	carrots
des petits pois	peas *(little peas)*
des haricots verts	green beans
des champignons	mushrooms *(champions)*

des oignons	onions
des choux de Bruxelles	brussels sprouts
des fruits	fruit
des cerises	cherries
des fraises	strawberries
des framboises	raspberries
des raisins	grapes
des raisins secs	raisins *(dry grapes)*
des saucisses	sausages
des crêpes	pancakes
des bonbons	sweets
des fruits de mer	seafood
des moules	mussels
des crudités	raw vegetables

At the restaurant

j'ai faim	I'm hungry
réserver une table	to book a table
pour commencer	to begin with
comme plat principal	as a main dish
commander	to order
vous avez choisi ?	have you chosen ?
un repas	meal
l'addition	bill
le plat du jour	dish of the day
les plats régionaux	local dishes
service compris	service included
un pourboire	tip

le serveur	waiter
la serveuse	waitress
Garçon!	waiter!
saignant	rare
à point	medium
bien cuit	well done
le dessert	pudding
je prends	I'll have
Bon appétit!	enjoy your meal!

Body

le bras   arm

*(think: flex your biceps to show you are **bra**ve)*

la jambe   leg

*(think: messy breakfast-eater drops **jam** on leg)*

la tête   head

(think: the accent is like a little hat on a head)

les oreilles   ears

*(think: hear people shout "**ooray!**")*

les épaules   shoulders

(think: "*hey Paul!*" you slap his shoulder...)

le nez   nose

(think: horse with long nose saying "**neigh**")

les dents   teeth

*(think: **dent**ist)*

le dos (pronounced "doh")   back

*(think: **back door** sounds like back – dos)*

la main   hand

*(think: the **main thing** you need to do anything)*

le pied	foot

*(think: « **pied**estrian »)*

la bouche	mouth
les yeux	eyes
le ventre / l'estomac	stomach
les genoux	knees
les joues	cheeks
la cheville	ankle

Health

La santé	health
garder la forme	to keep fit
rester en bonne santé	to stay healthy
il faut / on doit	one must
manger sainement	to eat healthily
manger équilibré	eat a balanced diet
s'entrainer	to train
faire du sport	to do sport
éviter le sucre	to avoid sugar
la malbouffe	junk food
bien que ce soit bon	although it's tasty
bouger	to move around
je fais un régime	I'm on a diet
il ne faut pas	one should not
ça fait grossir	it makes you fat

fumer	to smoke
se droguer	to take drugs
boire de l'alcool	to drink alcohol
devenir accro	to get addicted
déprimé	depressed
prévenir	to prevent
de graves maladies	serious illnesses
l'obésité	obesity
le sida	AIDS
de plus en plus de	more and more
le cancer de poumons	lung cancer
les crises cardiaques	heart attacks
des comprimés	pills
tousser	to cough
j'ai mal à la tête / au bras	my head / arm hurts
je me suis cassé la jambe	I broke my leg
un rhume	a cold
je suis enrhumé	I have a cold
la grippe	flu

Clothes

je porte	I wear
je mets	I put on
des vêtements	clothes
on doit porter	we have to wear
un uniforme	uniform

> **Top tip:** Think about a man wearing the masculine clothes and a woman wearing the feminine clothes. It's a bit unfair, because just as with the house vocab, she gets a lot more than he does, even the shirt, tie, jacket, socks and shoes. He gets jeans, trousers, a Tshirt, a jumper, coat, hat and gloves.

Masculine clothes

un pull	jumper *(pullover)*
un t-shirt	Tshirt
un jean	jeans
un pantalon	trousers *(pants long)*
un manteau	coat *(man, down to his toes)*
un chapeau	hat *(for a chap)*
un imperméable	raincoat
un bonnet	woolly hat
un casque	helmet

Feminine clothes

une veste	jacket *(not vest!)*
une robe	dress
une jupe	skirt
une chemise	shirt
une cravate	tie
une casquette	cap *(small helmet)*
une écharpe	scarf

Plural clothes

des chaussettes (f)	socks *(you need a set)*
des chaussures (f)	shoes *(be sure of them)*
des bottes (f)	boots
des baskets (f)	trainers
des gants (m)	gloves

Materials

en coton	cotton
en laine	wool
en soie	silk
en cuir	leather

Accessories

des écouteurs	earphones *(from écouter)*
des bijoux	jewellery
des lunettes	glasses
du maquillage	make-up
un portable	mobile
un parapluie	umbrella
des boucles d'oreille	earrings
un collier	necklace
un porte-monnaie	purse
un porte-feuille	wallet

Colours

Une couleur	a colour
rouge	red
orange	orange
jaune	yellow
vert(e)	green
bleu(e)	blue
rose	pink
violet	purple
blanc (blanche)	white
noir(e)	black
marron (*no plural*)	brown (chestnut)
gris(e)	grey

Animals

un chien	a dog
un chat	a cat
un lapin	a rabbit
une vache	a cow
un cheval	a horse
un mouton	a sheep
un cochon	a pig
un cochon d'inde	a guinea pig
un serpent	a snake
un cheval (des chevaux)	a horse
un poisson	a fish

J'ai un chien **qui** s'appelle	I have a dog called
Je n'ai pas **de** chien	I don't have a dog
Je n'ai pas **d'**animaux	I don't have a pet
Je voudrais **un** chien	I would like a dog
J'adore **les** chiens	I love dogs

Time phrases

Il est neuf heures moins le quart	8.45
Il est deux heures et demie	2.30
Il est huit heures et quart	8.15
Il est trois heures vingt	3.20
Il est onze heures moins vingt	10.40
à minuit	at midnight
à midi	at midday
hier	yesterday
demain	tomorrow
après avoir mangé	after eating
de temps en temps	sometimes
tous les jours	every day
le samedi	on Saturdays
la semaine dernière	last week *(note the e on both)*
l'année dernière	last year *(note the e on both)*
Le week-end dernier	last weekend *(no e or accent)*
le mois dernier	last month *(no e or accent)*
la semaine prochaine	next week *(note the e on both)*
l'année prochaine	next year *(note the e on both)*

Days of the week

lundi	Monday
mardi	Tuesday
mercredi	Wednesday
jeudi	Thursday
vendredi	Friday *(get the van ready)*
samedi	Saturday
dimanche	Sunday
lundi	on Monday
le lundi	on Mondays
Le week-end	at the weekend

Months of the year *(no capitals in French)*

janvier	January
février	February
mars	March
avril	April
mai	May
juin	June
juillet	July
août	August
septembre	September
octobre	October
novembre	November
décembre	December

Seasons

au printemps	in Spring *("oh! it's Spring!")*
en été	in Summer
en automne	in Autumn
en hiver	in Winter
à Pâques	at Easter
à Noël	at Christmas
le Toussaint	All-saints (October half-term)
Pentecôte	Whitsun (Summer half-term)

Negative expressions

Je ne mange pas	I don't eat
Je ne mange jamais	I never eat
Je ne mange plus	I no longer eat
Je ne mange que	I only eat
Je ne mange rien	I don't eat anything
Je ne vois personne	I don't see anyone
Personne ne le fait	Nobody does it
Il n'y a personne	there's nobody there
Je n'ai aucune idée	I have no idea

Grave accent words

There aren't many of these in words that are commonly used, but don't lose marks unnecessarily by forgetting the ones you should know.

après	after
très	very
près de	near
mère / père	mother, father
frère	brother
derrière	last
derrière	behind
à (eg à gauche / à Londres)	at / to (on the left)
où	where
là	there
Je me lève	I get up
J'espère	I hope
J'achète	I buy
Je préfère (sad eyebrow accents)	I prefer
problème	problem
déjà	already
élève	pupil
collège	school
bibliothèque	library
matière	subject
complètement	completely
mystère	mystery

Here's a story to help you remember the words :

Where do I live? I live **there**, in a **very** big house **near** London **behind** the **library**, with my **mother**, **father**, **brother**, **grandmother** and **grandfather**. I hope that when I **get up, I buy** something - but the **problem** is that I have to go to **school** and be a **pupil already** studying a **subject** and I **prefer** it to be **completely** a **mystery**

Using that story, see how many grave accent words you can remember and write them below:

Very french things

Some places and activities are peculiar to the French.

un Parisien	person from Paris
le TGV	train grande vitesse (fast train)
le SNCF	French railway company
le VTT	mountain biking
les randonnées	hikes
la chasse	hunting
la boulangerie	baker's shop
la pâtisserie	cake shop
quinze jours	a fortnight
le lycée	sixth form college
un lycéen	a sixth former
un département	similar to a "county" of France
les escargots	snails
en seconde	in year 12
en terminale	in year 13
redoubler	to repeat a year at school
le brevet	GCSE equivalent
un stage en entreprise	a work placement
préparer le bac	to do A levels
une commune	a village
la mairie	the town hall
faire la bise	to kiss on both cheeks
La Marseillaise	the national anthem
le tricolore	the French flag

Thank you for purchasing this book. I hope it has been helpful. If so, I would be very grateful if you would give the book a review on Amazon.

If you have any questions, please do contact me through my website **www.lucymartintuition.co.uk**

You may also be interested in my other books, also available on Amazon:

How to Ace your French Oral

French Vocabulary for GCSE

How to Ace your Spanish Oral

French Vocabulary for GCSE

How to Ace your German Oral

Brush up your French

Ten magic tricks with French

The A level French handbook

Spanish in a week

The Spanish GCSE Handbook

The Common Entrance French Handbook

Advanced French Vocabulary

Advanced French Conversation

Printed in Great Britain
by Amazon